EAT
YOURSELF
SMART

EAT YOURSELF SMART

INGREDIENTS & RECIPES
TO BOOST YOUR BRAIN POWER

GILL PAUL
NUTRITIONIST: KAREN SULLIVAN, ASET, VTCT, BSC

hamlyn

An Hachette UK Company
www.hachette.co.uk

First published in Great Britain in 2016 by Hamlyn,
a division of Octopus Publishing Group Ltd
Carmelite House
50 Victoria Embankment
London EC4Y 0DZ

Distributed in the US by
Hachette Book Group
1290 Avenue of the Americas
4th and 5th Floors
New York, NY 10020

Distributed in Canada by
Canadian Manda Group
664 Annette Street
Toronto, Ontario, Canada M6S 2C8

ISBN 978-0-600-63086-9

Printed and bound in China

10 9 8 7 6 5 4 3 2

All reasonable care has been taken in the preparation
of this book but the information it contains is not
intended to take the place of treatment by a qualified
medical practitioner.

This book includes dishes made with nuts and nut
derivatives. It is advisable for those with known
allergic reactions to nuts and nut derivatives and those
who may be potentially vulnerable to these allergies
to avoid dishes made with nuts and nut oils. It is also
prudent to check the labels of preprepared ingredients
for the possible inclusion of nut derivatives.

Ovens and broilers should be preheated to the
specified temperature—if using a convection oven,
follow the manufacturer's instructions for adjusting
the time and temperature.

Medium eggs should be used unless otherwise stated.

Some of the recipes in this book have previously
appeared in other titles published by Hamlyn.

Assistant Editor: Meri Pentikäinen
Art Director: Jonathan Christie
**Photographic Art Direction, Prop Styling
and Design:** Isabel de Cordova
Photography: Will Heap
Food Styling: Annie Nichols
Picture Library Manager: Jen Veall
Assistant Production Manager: Caroline Alberti

CONTENTS

INTRODUCTION

If you could take a magic pill to make you smarter, one that didn't have any unwanted side effects, would you take it? Imagine that it improves memory, and helps you solve problems, think on your feet, as well as maintain concentration for longer. Before long, everyone would want this pill and no doubt it would soon be sold out— but you can take your own magic pill for smartness just by choosing the right foods to boost your brain power.

Your brain is a mass of fat and water, about the size of your clenched fists held together with wrists touching, and it contains around 100 billion neurons, or brain cells. Multiple fingerlike dendrites reach out from each neuron toward other neurons, and as we think or move or speak, electrical impulses trigger the release of chemicals, known as neurotransmitters, to carry information from one neuron to the next.

Neurotransmitters help the brain form new connections as we absorb information, and they also connect memories that are visual, emotional, verbal, and physical. They evolve continually, with old, unused connections disappearing over time while new ones are formed. So, for optimum functioning of the brain, we require optimum levels of these neurotransmitters, which are manufactured in the brain from the foods that we eat.

What does the brain need?

A balanced mixture of proteins, vitamins, fats, minerals, and phytonutrients is needed for healthy brain functioning. Neurons are vulnerable to degenerative damage or oxidation, during which cells known as free radicals are produced. Smoking, drinking alcohol, pollution, exposure to sunlight, stress, and aging all increase the production of free radicals. However, antioxidants that are found in our food can not only protect the neurons but also reverse the damage, and they will form a key part of any eating plan designed to make you smarter. They can also help stave off Alzheimer's disease and dementia, and so they are well worth including in your daily diet.

Blood brings oxygen to the brain, as well as glucose to provide the energy to fuel all its processes and to supply the nutrients that are required to manufacture those vital neurotransmitters. A diet that encourages heart health will protect the blood supply to the brain, as will regular exercise, which pushes up the heart rate.

All-important hydration

- Aside from food, one of the most important things for getting your brain working to its full potential is water. Neurons store little droplets of water inside them, and these stop the brain from overheating, as well as keeping cell membranes elastic and able to do their job. By the time you actually feel thirsty, your brain is already functioning at a less than optimum level.

- Dehydration leads to fatigue, poor concentration, reduced ability to solve problems, and dizziness. However, drinking water regularly throughout the day will help to keep those neurons replenished and firing off connections with other neurons, so those brilliant ideas will just keep flooding out of you!

How to eat yourself smart

1. Choose the right fats

Sixty percent of the brain is made of fat, a high concentration of which is an omega-3 fat called DHA (docosahexaenoic acid), which is essential for the brain's processes. Our bodies don't produce the DHA we need so it all has to come from our diet, and the main source is oily fish, such as mackerel, salmon, sardines, herring, and trout. It can also be found in nuts (especially walnuts), eggs, seeds (flax seeds are great), whole grains, and dark-green leafy vegetables. Cut down on saturated fats (found in red meat) and avoid transfats (also known as hydrogenated fats), which are used in many processed foods. These can take the place of good fats in the brain and cause the membranes to become less flexible and the transmission of information more sluggish.

2. Pick plenty of proteins

Proteins contain the amino acids needed for the manufacture of those important neurotransmitters. Tyrosine (found in eggs, poultry, dairy products, leafy greens, and legumes) and tryptophan (in turkey, seeds, shellfish, nuts, and cocoa) are crucial.

Healthy proteins are required to build and maintain every cell in the body and are also essential for sustained energy.

3. Balance your blood sugar

Foods that cause your blood-sugar levels to peak and then plummet play havoc with concentration. If you have a Danish pastry or a sugary cereal for breakfast, you will experience a mid-morning slump and the temptation will be to reach for something sweet as a pick-me-up. It's not just sugary foods that have this effect, because refined carbohydrates, in which the whole-grain element has been stripped away, are quickly converted to blood sugar, too, as is alcohol. Opting for whole-grain carbohydrates, which are absorbed more slowly, will avoid this peaking and plummeting effect, as will eating protein along with fiber.

4. Aim for eight a day

The advice used to be to aim to eat five portions of fruit and vegetables every day, but nutritionists now think eight portions will give better protection. Remember to vary your choices, since they all contain different antioxidants to protect the brain from damage. However, the flavonoids in blueberries, black grapes, and strawberries are particular superstars in guarding against memory loss, while beets and leafy green vegetables help improve the blood supply to the brain.

5. Pump the iron!

Iron is vital for the supply of oxygenated blood to the brain, so an iron deficiency can affect memory, learning, and attention. Eating lean meats, shellfish, nuts and seeds, whole grains, dark chocolate, and leafy greens (especially spinach) on a regular basis will keep you well stocked with iron.

6. Make room for magnesium

Magnesium helps speed up the transmission of signals in the brain and relaxes the blood vessels to allow greater flow. Good sources include spinach, nuts, avocados, brown rice, and natural yogurt.

7. Bring on the B vitamins

High levels of the amino acid homocysteine can cause the brain to shrink but studies have shown that B vitamins, especially B_{12}, can protect against this. Meat, eggs, fish, and poultry are great sources, while leafy green vegetables, beans, and legumes also contain some.

Getting started

Normally it takes a few weeks to see beneficial results from a new healthy eating plan, but you'll notice a difference immediately when you start following the *Eat Yourself Smart* meal planner on pages 30–33. Eating a protein- and fiber-based breakfast and avoiding blood-sugar peaks and dips will make you sharper and more focused during the morning; lunch with a good balance of protein, carbohydrates, and healthy fats will see you firing on all cylinders through the afternoon; and a balanced dinner (eaten early in the evening if possible) will help you get a good night's sleep: another prerequisite for maximum brain power. Getting some exercise every day, quitting smoking, and not drinking more than one alcoholic drink per day will also make a big difference.

If you have a specific problem, such as a poor attention span, an unreliable memory, or difficulty with mental agility (doing crosswords, for example), you can check the problem solver on pages 26–29 for key foods you should be focusing on. Pages 12–25 list the best brain foods, along with their benefits, and you'll find suggestions on how to incorporate them into your diet.

The brain is our most precious organ of all. It defines who we are and how we interact with the world. Taking care of your brain now will pay dividends both in the short term, as you apply your newly fired-up neurons to your work and relationships, and in the long term, helping you look forward to a super-smart old age.

SMART
SUPERFOODS

SUPERFOODS

Full of natural goodness, these powerhouse foods will stimulate the healthy functioning of your brain.

Avocados

- ✔ Improve memory and prevent dementia
- ✔ Enhance neurotransmitter health
- ✔ Improve circulation
- ✔ Balance blood-sugar levels
- ✔ Increase cognitive ability
- ✔ Lift mood and energy levels

Avocados are a source of sustained energy to keep blood-sugar levels steady and raise mood and concentration levels. They are great for the body's own detoxification processes, which aid brain health.

They are rich in...

- → Oleic acid, which builds up myelin in the brain to help information travel faster, and lowers blood pressure
- → Folic acid, which reduces the risk of nerve tangles, a feature of Alzheimer's
- → Pantothenic acid and vitamin K to lower stress and improve the nervous system
- → Vitamin E, which neutralizes free radicals and reverses memory loss

Use in... leafy green salads, because avocados increase the uptake of nutrients by up to 200 percent; guacamole with crudités or wholegrain crackers; smoothies for an energizing snack or breakfast; on top of baked potatoes; sandwiches with tuna and olives; tomato and onion salads.

SEE: BLUEBERRY & AVOCADO SMOOTHIE, P38; SCRAMBLED EGGS & SMOKED SALMON, P50; BALSAMIC AVOCADO & STRAWBERRIES, P54; APPLE, AVOCADO & SPINACH SALAD, P76; CHOCOLATE AVOCADO PUDDING, P118.

Blueberries

✔ Reverse brain aging
✔ Improve cognitive function and mental agility
✔ Enhance heart health and circulation
✔ Reduce the impact of stress
✔ Increase decision-making, reasoning, verbal, and numerical skills
✔ Improve energy levels

Blueberries have a dramatic effect on the brain, both long and short term. One study found that drinking blueberry juice daily boosts memory by 30 percent. Blueberries also improve learning at any age and ward off Alzheimer's and Parkinson's disease.

They are rich in...

→ Flavonoids, which improve cognitive abilities such as reasoning, decision-making, learning, and motor skills
→ Antioxidants, which reduce the risk of dementia, stimulate the flow of blood to the brain, increase heart health, balance blood sugar, and lower blood pressure
→ Vitamin C, to boost immunity and lessen the effect of the stress hormone cortisol
→ Selenium, vitamins A and E, B-complex vitamins, zinc, and copper, which help heal damaged brain and nerve cells

Use in... smoothies; fresh or frozen; lightly cooked with a little honey to serve with yogurt, pancakes, or wholegrain toast; cakes or muffins; salads with feta and walnuts; fruity tagines and fruit crisps; fresh, chilled blueberry soup.

SEE: WHOLEWHEAT BLUEBERRY PANCAKES, P39; SPICED FRENCH FRUIT BREAD, P42; BLUEBERRY & AVOCADO SMOOTHIE, P38; BLUEBERRY & FLAX SEED BREAD, P64; BLUEBERRY & DATE MOUSSE, P122; FROZEN BERRY YOGURT, P123; FRUIT PARCELS & PISTACHIO YOGURT, P120.

Strawberries

✔ Improve learning
✔ Enhance long- and short-term memory
✔ Ease depression
✔ Improve alertness and concentration
✔ Reduce the impact of stress on the brain
✔ Help to prevent dementia

Strawberries are a fantastic source of antioxidants that can prevent age-related brain decline and help protect the brain and nerve cells from free radicals. They have been shown to enhance learning and improve short- and long-term memory.

They are rich in...

→ Fisetin compounds, which build long-term memory and improve short-term memory and intellectual performance in a short period of time
→ Anthocyanidins, flavonoids that are found in the learning and memory parts of the brain, and protect brain neurons linked with memory
→ Vitamin C to boost immunity, aid neural pathways, and reduce the impact of cortisol, the stress hormone
→ Selenium, vitamins A and E, B-complex vitamins, zinc, and copper, which all help heal damaged brain and nerve cells

Use in... fruit crisps with rhubarb; with yogurt and toasted oats for a tasty parfait; chilled soups; smoothies and pressed fruit juices; with sugar and balsamic vinegar; fruit salads or leafy green salads with pears, lightly toasted walnuts and goat cheese; pancakes; on oat crackers with cream cheese.

SEE: SPICED FRENCH FRUIT BREAD, P42; BALSAMIC AVOCADO & STRAWBERRIES, P54; STRAWBERRY & GRAPE SMOOTHIE, P36; FROZEN BERRY YOGURT, P123; FRUIT PARCELS & PISTACHIO YOGURT, P120; CHOCOLATE-DIPPED STRAWBERRIES, P116.

Black grapes

✔ Encourage healthy brain cells and neurotransmitter networks
✔ Improve memory and concentration
✔ Balance blood sugar
✔ Promote cognitive abilities
✔ Promote heart health and circulation
✔ Prevent dementia
✔ Reduce toxicity and inflammation
✔ Enhance mental agility

Black, red, and purple grapes and their seeds are among the best brain superfoods, and they have health benefits for the heart, too. Their juice doesn't contain fiber, as the whole fruit does, but it will provide crucial antioxidant support for your brain.

They are rich in...

→ Antioxidants and other compounds that aid brain-cell renewal, strengthen connections in the memory part of the brain, and prevent cognitive decline
→ Resveratrol, known for aiding circulation, which reduces dementia by bringing oxygen and nutrients to the brain
→ Minerals manganese and potassium, which lower blood pressure, boost immunity, and prevent depression
→ Fiber, to balance blood sugar, fight toxins and inflammation, aid nutrient absorption, and retain energy for better concentration and attention span

Use in... smoothies and juices; frozen as a sweet snack; chicken salads with nuts and leafy greens; muesli and granola with live yogurt, oats, and maple syrup; tarts and fruit salads; Caesar or Waldorf salads.

SEE: STRAWBERRY & GRAPE SMOOTHIE, P36; MUESLI WITH HONEY & GRAPES, P47; QUAILS WITH GINGER & GRAPES, P98; BEAN BURGERS WITH PECAN COLESLAW, P109.

Granny Smith apples

✔ Balance blood sugar
✔ Boost alertness and concentration
✔ Provide energy and ease stress
✔ Increase cognition
✔ Prevent dementia
✔ Lower toxicity

Apples can help to prevent and to halt Alzheimer's and other forms of dementia, as well as improve memory and cognitive function. Granny Smiths have the highest levels of phenols of all apples and are less acidic. They are also high in antioxidants, which slow down the degenerative effects of aging.

They are rich in...

→ Flavonoids, which reduce damage to neurons and inhibit harmful genes that can lead to dementia
→ Boron, which improves the transmission of messages across the central nervous system, while stimulating brain cells
→ Catechins, which protect the brain from harmful chemicals
→ Quercetin, which reduces stress, protects brain cells from cognitive decline, and encourages mental activity

Use in... salads with goat cheese and dried apricots; stuffed into whole chicken breasts with walnuts, thyme, and quinoa or oats; pork roasts; baked and stuffed with raisins, honey, and cinnamon; coleslaws; berry crisps with a nutty, oaty topping; smoothies or fruit juices.

SEE: APPLE CINNAMON PORRIDGE, P40; APPLE & WALNUT SQUARES, P44; BEAN BURGERS WITH PECAN COLESLAW, P109; HERBED APPLE COMPOTE, P70; APPLE, AVOCADO & SPINACH SALAD, P76; APPLE & NUTMEG SMOOTHIE, P68; APPLE, MAPLE & PECAN WHIP, P124; CINNAMON-BAKED APPLES, P119.

Coffee

- ✔ Lifts mood
- ✔ Enhances alertness
- ✔ Promotes cognitive function
- ✔ Improves memory
- ✔ Encourages neurotransmitter health
- ✔ Promotes mental agility
- ✔ Lifts energy levels
- ✔ Helps prevent dementia

Coffee has, over the years, had a fairly mixed press, with its caffeine content being blamed for exacerbating the symptoms of stress and anxiety, and suggestions that it robs the body of key nutrients. However, we do know that, in moderation, coffee can make you smarter, thanks largely to the effects it has on brain activity.

It's rich in...

- → Caffeine, to block the neurotransmitter adenosine, which promotes sleepiness and suppresses arousal; caffeine can also improve reaction time, memory, and cognitive function, while promoting the release of dopamine, the mood-lifting neurotransmitter
- → Antioxidants, which can reduce the risk of developing Alzheimer's and block inflammation in the brain
- → B vitamins (riboflavin and pantothenic acid), to support the nervous system and encourage the processing of information in the brain

Use in... spicy stews, casseroles, tagines, chili con carne, and other meaty dishes to deepen flavor; add to chocolate desserts; create delicious granitas; rub into pork and other meats; flavor cakes, custards, and cheesecakes; serve chilled on ice with a pinch of cinnamon and a splash of vanilla; or simply drink two or three cups of good-quality black coffee every day to access the health benefits.

SEE: ESPRESSO & CHILI PORK TENDERLOIN, P100; COFFEE POTS, P112; COFFEE & WALNUT CAKE, P114; COFFEE GRANITA & VANILLA YOGURT, P110.

Dark chocolate

- ✔ Improves mental agility and cognition
- ✔ Balances blood-sugar levels and mood
- ✔ Enhances memory
- ✔ Reduces stress hormones
- ✔ Improves circulation
- ✔ Beats fatigue
- ✔ Increases alertness and concentration
- ✔ Promotes neurotransmitter health
- ✔ Helps prevent dementia

Dark chocolate encourages health and well-being on all levels. It boosts the circulatory system to encourage blood flow to the brain, improving cognitive function, and even math skills. Eaten in moderation it's the perfect addition to a smart diet.

It's rich in...

- → Flavonols to boost circulation and promote blood flow to the brain, while encouraging optimal cell function
- → A wide range of other antioxidants to promote overall heart and brain health and protect the cells from damage caused by free radicals and aging
- → Phenylethylamine (PEA), which releases endorphins, the feel-good chemicals, and enhances cognition
- → Caffeine, to boost alertness, energy, mood, and cognitive function

Use in... curries and chilies to lift flavor; on fresh fruit, breakfast cereals, or yogurt; nibble a few squares as a snack or a treat; melt and mix in a handful of fruit and nuts; melt and stir into a few tablespoons of plain yogurt with a drop of vanilla for an instant chocolate sauce; cakes and pastries.

SEE: BLUEBERRY & DATE MOUSSE, P122; ORANGE & CHOCOLATE TART, P115; CHOCOLATE-DIPPED STRAWBERRIES, P116; CHOCOLATE AVOCADO PUDDING, P118.

Live yogurt

- ✔ Reduces blood pressure
- ✔ Increases the absorption of B vitamins
- ✔ Enables restful sleep
- ✔ Eases anxiety and lifts mood
- ✔ Enhances cognitive function and focus
- ✔ Promotes neurotransmitter action

Live yogurt is rich in the healthy bacteria that enhance immunity and the health of the gut. A source of calming calcium, it aids restful sleep and eases anxiety, while promoting the health of the brain and nervous system.

It's rich in...

- → Probiotics, which relieve stress, anxiety, and depression, and help decision-making and cognitive function
- → B vitamins, to ensure a healthy nervous system and aid relaxation
- → Amino acids, for brain development and growth, better concentration, and balanced blood-sugar levels
- → Magnesium, which helps the brain with mental tasks, concentration, alertness, and cognition, and helps reduce fatigue

Use in... smoothies; muesli; on top of baked potatoes; dips with chives, lemon zest, and black pepper; served with desserts and cakes, with a drop of vanilla; soups; salad dressing with cilantro and orange zest.

SEE: MUESLI WITH HONEY & GRAPES, P47; WHOLE-WHEAT BLUEBERRY PANCAKES, P39; SCRAMBLED EGGS & SMOKED SALMON, P50; SPICED FRENCH FRUIT BREAD, P42; APPLE & NUTMEG SMOOTHIE, P68; KIDNEY BEAN DIP & FLAX CRACKERS, P57; SPICY CHICKEN WITH LEMON RICE, P94; BEAN BURGERS WITH PECAN COLESLAW, P109; APPLE, AVOCADO & SPINACH SALAD, P76; FALAFELS WITH BEET SALAD, P77; FRUIT PACKAGES & PISTACHIO YOGURT, P120; COFFEE GRANITA & VANILLA YOGURT, P110; FROZEN BERRY YOGURT, P123.

Eggs

✔ Balance blood-sugar levels
✔ Increase cognition and memory
✔ Reduce stress and anxiety
✔ Prevent age-related decline
✔ Promote neurotransmitter health
✔ Reduce risk of dementia
✔ Provide energy
✔ Boost concentration and attention span

Eggs are some of the most nutritionally balanced foods in the world, so it shouldn't surprise that they are also great for the brain. They can help prevent age-related changes in the brain, while promoting brain health at cell and message-carrying level. Moreover, they supply a sustained source of energy that can encourage concentration and mental agility, while balancing moods and regulating stress.

They are rich in...

➔ Vitamin B$_{12}$, which guards against the type of brain shrinkage that can lead to dementia, poor memory, and Alzheimer's disease

➔ Choline, which is essential for the development of brain cells to enhance memory, cognitive function, and mental agility, and is a precursor for the neurotransmitter acetylcholine, necessary for short-term memory

➔ Essential fatty acids, which prevent age-related degeneration and nourish the brain, while facilitating connections between neurons

➔ Tyrosine, which promotes mental activity and concentration

Use in... omelets and scrambled eggs with spinach and smoked salmon, topped with fresh chives and dill; boil for an easy, nutritious breakfast or snack; poach and serve on a bed of steamed leafy greens; stir into fried rice dishes or add to sauces; boil, chop, and mix with live yogurt, scallions, and freshly ground black pepper for a sandwich filling or a light meal.

SEE: SPICED FRENCH FRUIT BREAD, P42; SCRAMBLED EGG ENCHILADAS, P48; FRIED EGGS WITH SAGE, P51; SCRAMBLED EGGS & SMOKED SALMON, P50; APPLE & WALNUT SQUARES, P44; ASPARAGUS WITH SMOKED SALMON, P85; BUTTERNUT, CHARD & HERB TART, P82; BELL PEPPER, FETA & EGG TAGINE, P92; COFFEE & WALNUT CAKE, P114; ORANGE & CHOCOLATE TART, P115.

Flax seeds

✔ Encourage brain development
✔ Prevent age-related degeneration
✔ Help with information processing
✔ Improve memory
✔ Boost concentration and mental agility
✔ Balance blood sugar
✔ Lift mood

A source of omega-3 fatty acids, flax seeds improve memory, lift mood, and help you concentrate for longer. Regular intake can prevent age-related memory loss and build and maintain connections between neurons in the brain.

They are rich in...

→ Omega-3 oils, required to build and protect neurons, facilitate transmission of messages, and activate the cerebral cortex where information is processed; and enhance concentration
→ Phenylalanine, required for the production of dopamine, which lifts mood and helps sustain attention
→ Fiber for heart and brain health, while improving digestion, the uptake of nutrients, and sustained energy levels
→ Lignans, which are a great source of protective antioxidants

Use in... breakfast cereals or muesli; use the oil in salad dressings and marinades; ground seeds in smoothies; whole seeds in baked goods; soak in boiling water or hot fruit juice and use as the basis for a porridge topped with fruit, maple syrup, nuts, and live yogurt; casseroles, soups, and stews; burgers.

SEE: APRICOT & PRUNE MUESLI, P46; MUESLI WITH HONEY & GRAPES, P47; BLUEBERRY & FLAX SEED BREAD, P64; SMOKED SALMON & EDAMAME CUPS, P52; KIDNEY BEAN DIP & FLAX CRACKERS, P57; BUTTERNUT, CHARD & HERB TART, P82.

Oats

✔ Lift mood and reduce anxiety
✔ Boost neurotransmitter health
✔ Balance blood sugar
✔ Improve attention span
✔ Raise energy
✔ Enhance cognitive ability
✔ Prevent dementia and other age-related conditions

A "grain for the brain," oats are a powerful superfood that improves your memory and cognitive ability and boosts your attention, concentration, mood, energy, and alertness. Oats also contain soluble fiber, lowering cholesterol, which can damage the brain.

They are rich in...

→ B vitamins to support a healthy nervous system and reduce the risk of cognitive decline, while improving data processing and memory
→ Vitamin E, which protects the brain from age-related decline
→ Potassium, which encourages the supply of oxygen to the brain, nourishes the nervous system, and helps reduce stress and anxiety
→ Manganese, necessary to process brain nutrients choline and thiamine

Use in... porridge with fresh fruit and nuts; toast and sprinkle over salads and soups; oat crackers with hummus or nut butters; topping for fish pie, and fruit or vegetable crisps; as a coating for baked fish or chicken; Irish soda bread, served with smoked salmon and dill.

SEE: APRICOT & PRUNE GRANOLA, P46; APPLE CINNAMON PORRIDGE, P40; MUESLI WITH HONEY & GRAPES, P47; APPLE & WALNUT SQUARES, P44; CHEWY OAT & RAISIN BARS, P71; COCOA, ORANGE & PECAN OATBARS, P66.

Brown rice

✔ Boosts memory
✔ Balances blood sugar
✔ Aids brain development
✔ Encourages neurotransmitter health
✔ Lowers levels of toxicity
✔ Increases energy levels
✔ Enhances concentration and alertness
✔ Balances mood
✔ Eases anxiety and symptoms of stress
✔ Lowers blood pressure

Brown rice is a source of fiber. It clears out waste products, which can impact mood, memory, energy levels, and concentration, and ensures that nutrients are absorbed better. It also helps reduce blood sugar- and mood swings, all of which encourage focus and increased cognitive powers.

It's rich in...

→ Gamma aminobutyric acid (GABA), a neurotransmitter and memory-aider
→ B vitamins, which produce energy for the brain cells
→ Tryptophan, which increases serotonin and melatonin in the body to encourage well-being, relaxation, and restful sleep
→ Manganese, necessary to produce energy from protein and carbohydrates and synthesize fatty acids

Use in... soups, stews, and casseroles; rice puddings; risottos; salads with dried fruit, berries, cheeses, herbs, and leafy greens; stuffing, baked with broccoli, fresh and sun-dried tomatoes, cheese, and pine nuts; top with salsa, black beans, onions, avocado, and grated cheese for an easy Mexican meal; season with herbs, spices, and scallions.

SEE: CREMINI MUSHROOM PILAF, P103; SPICY CHICKEN WITH LEMON RICE, P94; RICE, PECAN & CRANBERRY SALAD, P72.

Kale

✔ Prevents dementia
✔ Aids neurotransmitter health
✔ Balances blood sugar
✔ Encourages restful sleep
✔ Provides energy and lifts mood
✔ Increases circulation
✔ Aids cognition and concentration
✔ Helps reverse the effects of aging

Kale is full of fiber and nutrients, including antioxidants and omega-3 oils, which support brain health and even help reverse some of the degenerative effects of aging.

It's rich in...

→ Sulforaphane, to encourage liver health and remove toxins from the blood
→ Omega-3 fatty acids, which lower the risk of depression, promote circulation and healthy blood vessels, discourage inflammation, and support nerve health
→ Vitamin K, which protects and produces the fats that structure the brain
→ Vitamin B_6, iron, and folic acid, required for neurotransmitters, balanced mood and energy levels, memory, and focus
→ L-tyrosine, which is needed for neurotransmitters that aid problem-solving, learning, and memory

Use in... soups, stews, casseroles, and stir-fries; roasted with olive oil; omelets or scrambled eggs; steam with lemon zest, olive oil, and black pepper; salads with mango, walnuts, pomegranate seeds, and blueberries, with an orange and honey vinaigrette; Caesar salads.

SEE: SMOKED HADDOCK & KALE SOUP, P86; RICE, PECAN & CRANBERRY SALAD, P72; LAMB WITH KALE & SPICY TOMATO SALSA, P102; SPAGHETTI WITH KALE & TOMATOES, P106; FRAGRANT VEGETARIAN CHILI, P104.

Kidney beans

- ✔ Lift mood
- ✔ Lengthen attention span
- ✔ Enhance concentration
- ✔ Balance blood sugar
- ✔ Reduce toxicity and inflammation
- ✔ Encourage restful sleep
- ✔ Ease stress
- ✔ Provide energy
- ✔ Improve memory

All types of legumes are considered to be "brain food," not only because they are rich in brain-building proteins and B vitamins, but also because they provide a sustained source of energy to help lift mood, promote concentration and a longer attention span, and encourage restful sleep. Red kidney beans also contain antioxidants, which can slow down the degenerative effects of aging—in all parts of the body.

They are rich in...

- → Vitamin K, which supports the brain and nervous system, and produces the fats necessary for brain construction
- → Thiamine, a B vitamin crucial for cognitive function and the prevention of dementia
- → Soluble fiber to balance blood sugar and mood, and enhance energy levels, concentration, and alertness
- → Iron to increase energy levels and ensure the ready supply of oxygenated blood to the brain

Use in... dips served with whole-grain crackers and crudités; add to Mexican burritos, enchiladas, and chilis; use in soups, stews, curries, and casseroles; toss into salads and garlicky pasta dishes; bake with maple syrup, smoked bacon, and tomatoes; add to pilaf rice.

SEE: KIDNEY BEAN DIP & FLAX CRACKERS, P57; SPICY MIXED BEAN SALSA, P56; BEAN BURGERS WITH PECAN COLESLAW, P109; FRAGRANT VEGETARIAN CHILI, P104.

Beets

✔ Reduce blood pressure
✔ Increase energy
✔ Improve circulation
✔ Enhance memory
✔ Ward off dementia
✔ Boost concentration, attention span, alertness, and mental agility
✔ Balance mood and ease anxiety

The antioxidants in beets help ward off the degeneration that affects brain health. They also have an almost instant impact on blood pressure, which helps improve blood flow to the brain. Beets also contain great levels of iron, which oxygenates the blood.

They are rich in...

→ Nitrates, which expand the walls of the blood vessels so more energy, nutrients, and oxygen reach the brain, including those areas associated with dementia
→ B vitamins, required for data processing and memory, as well the health of the nervous system
→ Betalains, plant chemicals that have strong anti-inflammatory, detox, and antioxidant properties (inflammation is one of the precursors to memory loss)
→ Fiber for sustained energy and focus and balanced blood sugar

Use in... coleslaw or leafy green salads; on whole-grain bread with soft fresh cheese; juice with berries; borscht, topped with herby pita croutons; roast and purée with horseradish for an easy dip.

SEE: PARSNIP & BEET CHIPS, P58; BEET & HORSERADISH HUMMUS, P60; APPLE, AVOCADO & SPINACH SALAD, P76; BEET & MACKEREL LENTILS, P78; FALAFELS WITH BEET SALAD, P77; BAKED PUMPKIN, BEETS & CHEESE, P108.

Spinach

✔ Improves mood
✔ Aids memory and prevents dementia
✔ Promotes learning
✔ Improves neurotransmitter health
✔ Eases stress and anxiety
✔ Promotes mental agility
✔ Lowers levels of toxicity

Spinach is an exemplary food for the brain, halting cognitive decline, reducing anxiety and stress, encouraging restful sleep, and promoting mental agility and learning.

It's rich in...

→ B vitamins, which reduce the risk of age-related cognitive decline, enhance mood and memory, and help you relax
→ Vitamin E, to encourage the growth of new brain and nerve tissue, and the release of dopamine, which controls the flow of information in the brain
→ Antioxidants, which reduce age-related memory problems and motor deficits
→ Folates, which maintain healthy brain circulation, form neurotransmitters, protect DNA, and help the liver to detoxify the body and brain

Use in... soups, stews, casseroles, curries, tagines, and pasta sauces; salads with feta cheese, chopped eggs, avocado, grated beets, and a lemony yogurt dressing; as a bed for poached eggs or steamed fish; lightly wilt with cumin and lemon zest and serve with toasted pita; stuff into pork or chicken breasts; omelets and pasta shells.

SEE: SCRAMBLED EGG ENCHILADAS, P48; CHEESE ROULADE WITH SPINACH, P80; SPINACH TAPENADE WITH PAN-FRIED CHEESE, P84; APPLE, AVOCADO & SPINACH SALAD, P76; CREMINI MUSHROOM PILAF, P103; WALNUT-CRUSTED SALMON, P90.

Chard

✔ Improves concentration
✔ Prevents age-related decline
✔ Encourages better cognition
✔ Aids memory
✔ Promotes restful sleep
✔ Protects the brain
✔ Encourages neurotransmitter health

Chard is a terrific brain food that has been shown to help prevent Alzheimer's while promoting healthy brain function. Its high antioxidant content, as well as vitamins B and E, works to encourage brain function in both the short and long term.

It's rich in...

➔ B vitamins, including folic acid, known to decrease the risk of cognitive decline, while nourishing the nervous system
➔ Vitamin E, a potent antioxidant that protects the brain (and body) from free-radical damage
➔ Vitamin K, which protects the brain from damage to the neurons, while improving concentration; also used in the treatment of Alzheimer's
➔ Iron, which encourages the supply of oxygenated blood to the brain and improves energy levels, while helping to lower blood pressure

Use in... stir-fries, with a little olive or grapeseed oil to enhance absorption of key nutrients; lightly steam and toss into salads; finely chop and add to soups, omelets, curries, and casseroles; braise with lentils, lemon juice, and crispy bacon; serve as a gratin with leeks.

SEE: SPICY CHARD & BEAN SOUP, P88; BUTTER-NUT, CHARD & HERB TART, P82; ESPRESSO & CHILI PORK TENDERLOIN, P100.

Chiles

✔ Increase cognition
✔ Ease stress
✔ Prevent dementia and boost memory
✔ Aid concentration and attention
✔ Support mental agility
✔ Relieve anxiety
✔ Encourage neurotransmitter health
✔ Improve circulation

Fruits rather than vegetables, chiles are a great source of multiple vitamins and minerals. Chiles have even been linked to improved memory and reduced pain, and contain antioxidants required to support optimum brain health.

They are rich in...

➔ Vitamin B_6, which is required for essential brain activity and also helps balance mood
➔ Capsaicin, which releases endorphins to ease pain, increase concentration, lift mood, and reduce anxiety and stress
➔ Vitamin C for tissue repair, good circulation, healthy brain activity, and balanced mood
➔ Vitamin A, required for red blood cell formation, necessary for a good supply of oxygenated blood, as well as growth and development of the brain

Use in... curries, stir-fries, soups, stews, and casseroles; finely chop into omelets; roast, purée, and add to hummus; thinly slice over pasta or pizza; stuff with herby cream cheese or feta and roast; roast, purée, and spread on halloumi cheese; finely chop and add to macaroni and cheese or risotto.

SEE: SCRAMBLED EGG ENCHILADAS, P48; SPICY CHARD & BEAN SOUP, P88; BUTTERNUT, CHARD & HERB TART, P82; FRAGRANT VEGETARIAN CHILI, P104.

Sage

✔ Increases attention span
✔ Improves memory
✔ Improves circulation
✔ Enhances cognitive ability
✔ Prevents dementia
✔ Aids neurotransmitter health
✔ Improves mental agility

....

Sage can have a quite remarkable and near-instant impact on short-term memory and also, in the longer term, Alzheimer's. In fact, sage contains chemicals very similar to the drugs used to treat Alzheimer's.

....

It's rich in...

→ Phytochemicals to prevent the breakdown of the neurotransmitter acetylcholine, which is involved in learning, memory, and cognition
→ Rosmarinic acid, which reduces inflammation and acts as an antioxidant to protect the brain and nervous system
→ Superoxide dismutase (SOD), which stabilizes the brain cells and helps prevent damage from free radicals
→ Carnosic acid, to prevent free-radical damage and increase levels of glutathione, which improves circulation and is used to treat brain diseases, such as autism and Alzheimer's

....

Use in... savory stuffings; chicken and pork dishes; chop and scatter over pumpkin and squash curries, soups, pasta, and roasted vegetable dishes; tea with mint and lemon; finely chop and steep in olive oil with garlic, and then use to dress gnocchi; use to fill crêpes with smoked cheese and sliced baby leeks; add to omelets.

....

SEE: FRIED EGGS WITH SAGE, P51; PARSNIP, SAGE & CHESTNUT SOUP, P89; PECANS WITH BROWN BUTTER & SAGE, P62; HERBED APPLE COMPOTE, P70.

Pecans

✔ Lift mood
✔ Improve circulation
✔ Reduce inflammation
✔ Promote restful sleep
✔ Prevent dementia and improve memory
✔ Aid concentration and mental agility
✔ Reduce stress and anxiety
✔ Promote neurotransmitter health

....

The omega-3 fatty acids in pecans have been proven to encourage brain health on every level, and also work to reduce the risk of heart disease and diabetes, which damage the brain by reducing blood flow.

....

They are rich in...

→ Vitamin E, which prevents age-related mental decline and also protects the brain and nervous system from damage
→ Magnesium, which reduces anxiety and depression, and ensures a balance of chemicals in the brain
→ Omega-3 oils, which can reduce the risk of neural degeneration
→ Copper, which is required to make the neurotransmitter norepinephrine, used in communication; also needed to protect and aid message transmission

....

Use in... hot or cold breakfast cereals; as a base for pesto sauces, with pecorino cheese, cilantro, garlic, and olive oil; cookies, oatmeal bars, dark-chocolate brownies, and oaty energy bars; salads with fresh spinach, sliced pears, cranberries, and caramelized onions; ground as a coating for fleshy fish.

....

SEE: APPLE CINNAMON PORRIDGE, P40; COCOA, ORANGE & PECAN BARS, P66; PECANS WITH BROWN BUTTER & SAGE, P62; RICE, PECAN & CRANBERRY SALAD, P72; BEAN BURGERS WITH PECAN COLESLAW, P109; APPLE, MAPLE & PECAN WHIPS, P124.

Walnuts

- ✔ Improve learning and information processing
- ✔ Reduce cognitive decline
- ✔ Aid concentration and attention span
- ✔ Lift mood and relieve anxiety
- ✔ Improve circulation
- ✔ Encourage restful sleep
- ✔ Balance blood sugar
- ✔ Prevent dementia

Walnuts have the ability to reverse signs of aging and promote brain health, improve memory and motor skills. They're also high in protein, antioxidants, and omega-3 oils.

They are rich in...

- → Vitamin E, to reduce cognitive decline associated with aging
- → Omega-3 oils, which increase cognitive regeneration, improve memory, and raise melatonin levels to encourage sleep and relaxation; they also keep the brain fluid and flexible, largely because it is made up of structural fats
- → Folic acid, used for brain development and performance, balanced mood, and the prevention of dementia
- → Arginine, an amino acid used for cell division and the synthesis of protein

Use in... tossed with Gorgonzola cheese, spinach, olive oil, and pasta; pork or chicken stuffings with apples and sage; warm lentil salads with goat cheese; fruit or vegetable crisp toppings; wild rice salads and pilaf dishes; Belgian endive and apple salads; enjoy on their own, eaten as a snack.

SEE: APPLE & WALNUT SQUARES, P44; SMOKED DUCK & CLEMENTINE SALAD, P74; CHEESE ROULADE WITH SPINACH, P80; APPLE, AVOCADO & SPINACH SALAD, P76; WALNUT-CRUSTED SALMON, P90; COFFEE & WALNUT CAKE, P114.

Mackerel

- ✔ Boosts neurotransmitter health
- ✔ Lifts mood and boosts energy
- ✔ Eases inflammation
- ✔ Increases cognitive ability
- ✔ Aids memory and prevents dementia
- ✔ Balances blood sugar
- ✔ Promotes mental agility
- ✔ Enhances concentration

Mackerel has been shown to boost learning power and memory, and prevent age-related decline, in particular, conditions associated with dementia, brain shrinkage, and inflammation.

It's rich in...

- → Omega-3 oils, used by brain cells in communication and to reduce inflammation associated with cognitive decline; these oils also aid memory, mental performance, and emotional health
- → Vitamin B_{12} to enhance energy levels and protect against Alzheimer's
- → Co-enzyme Q10, which protects neurons and provides nourishment for cells
- → Vitamin D, to reduce inflammation and improve cognitive abilities and mood

Use in... fish cakes or watercress salads with new potatoes and a lemony dressing; enjoy it smoked, baked, or barbecued; serve on whole-grain bread with beets, lemon mayonnaise, and plenty of leafy greens; add to creamy fish pies; bake with leeks, serve with macaroni and cheese; brush with harissa and orange juice and fry in a skillet.

SEE: MACKEREL PÂTÉ & PITA BITES, P63; BEET & MACKEREL LENTILS, P78; GINGER & LIME MACKEREL, P95.

Wild salmon

- ✔ Improves behavioral problems
- ✔ Eases depression and anxiety
- ✔ Reduces cognitive decline
- ✔ Aids memory
- ✔ Balances mood
- ✔ Prevents dementia
- ✔ Promotes concentration and alertness
- ✔ Lifts energy levels

Wild salmon is a great source of omega-3 oils that are critical to brain health, but it also plays a vital role in overall health and well-being. Because it is nutrient-dense, it is an excellent source of high-quality protein that forms the building blocks of all the cells in the body, and helps stabilize blood-sugar levels and mood. Wild salmon is superior to farmed salmon because it contains fewer of the pesticides and chemicals associated with fish farming.

It's rich in...
- → Omega-3 oils, which ease inflammation, improve brain function, improve circulation, and boost the activity of the cerebral cortex, where information is processed
- → DHA, known to reduce depression and improve mood and cognition
- → Vitamin E, a powerful antioxidant that protects the brain from free radicals and age-related decline, while encouraging the release of dopamine to aid the flow of information within the brain
- → Tryptophan, which encourages relaxation, clearer thinking, restful sleep, and enhanced concentration

Use in... pasta dishes and risottos; serve alongside scrambled eggs, in omelets, or as a bed for poached eggs; flake into crisp vegetable salads; serve on rye bread with lemon mayonnaise; use in fish cakes or burgers; serve in sushi; top with walnut and cilantro pesto and bake in the oven; serve in a red Thai curry; broil with chile and lime butter.

SEE: SCRAMBLED EGGS & SMOKED SALMON, P50; SMOKED SALMON & EDAMAME CUPS, P52; ASPARAGUS WITH SMOKED SALMON, P85; CRISPY SALMON RAMEN, P96; WALNUT-CRUSTED SALMON, P90.

WHAT'S YOUR PROBLEM?

These functional foods target specific aspects of brain function, mood, and other areas of health that affect general smartness. Decide which symptoms you suffer from and choose from the foods and recipes that can relieve them. These icons are used throughout the recipe section to highlight which recipes can help combat which symptoms.

Poor concentration

Wild salmon, brown rice, avocados, trout, beets, flax seeds, black grapes, dark chocolate, Granny Smith apples, beans, chiles, mackerel, live yogurt, leafy green vegetables, green tea, bananas, pecans, eggs, oats, walnuts, berries, seaweed, sardines, sunflower seeds, broccoli, tomatoes, cabbage

Recipes include:
Scrambled eggs & smoked salmon, p50; Spicy chard & bean soup, p88; Herbed apple compote, p70; Walnut-crusted salmon, p90.

Short attention span

Beets, eggs, chiles, flax seeds, kidney beans, oats, sage, nuts, kale, Granny Smith apples, live yogurt, citrus fruits, carrots, fatty fish, mint, leafy green vegetables, blueberries, avocados

Recipes include:
Muesli with honey & grapes, p47; Apple & nutmeg smoothie, p68; Smoked duck & clementine salad, p74; Baked pumpkin, beets & cheese, p108.

Reduced alertness

Yogurt, legumes, oats, wild salmon, liver, avocados, beets, brown rice, coffee, soy, dark chocolate, Granny Smith apples, red bell peppers, eggs, pecans, walnuts, shellfish, leafy green vegetables, citrus fruits, berries, seeds, whole grains, mango, apricots

Recipes Include:
Kidney bean dip & flax crackers, p57; Cheese roulade with spinach, p80; Butternut, chard & herb tart, p82; Coffee desserts, p112.

Slow thinking

Beets, berries, coffee, black grapes, dark chocolate, eggs, flax seeds, chiles, oily fish, nuts, sage, pumpkin seeds, red wine, brown rice, black and green tea, oats, whole grains, sweet potatoes, dairy produce, leafy green vegetables, apples, olive oil, bananas

Recipes include:
Scrambled egg enchiladas, p48; Blueberry & flax seed bread, p64; Ginger & lime mackerel, p95; Blueberry & date mousse, p122.

Poor memory

Coffee, sunflower seeds, black grapes, dark chocolate, red cabbage, eggs, flax seeds, Granny Smith apples, chiles, olive oil, turmeric, oily fish, rosemary, leafy green vegetables, kidney beans, oats, pecans, sage, whole grains, quinoa, brown rice, walnuts, peanuts, avocados, beets, tomatoes

Recipes include:
Apple cinnamon porridge, p40; Rice, pecan & cranberry salad, p72; Walnut-crusted salmon, p90; Coffee & walnut cake, p114.

Low energy levels

Avocados, beets, brown rice, coffee, eggs, Granny Smith apples, apricots, live yogurt, blueberries, oats, mackerel, wild salmon, broccoli, quinoa, sesame and pumpkin seeds, kale, whole grains, chard, legumes, spinach, sprouted seeds, almonds, goji berries, walnuts

Recipes include:
Whole-wheat blueberry pancakes, p39; Chewy oat & raisin bars, p71; Smoked haddock & kale soup, p86; Spicy chicken with lemon rice, p94.

Low mood

Coffee, mushrooms, halibut, carrots, dark chocolate, melon, eggs, nuts, chiles, kale, kidney beans, sweet potatoes, live yogurt, kiwifruit, oats, bell peppers, apricots, mackerel, spinach, cinnamon, oranges, yeast, wild salmon, quinoa, cabbage, avocados, beets, whole grains

Recipes include:
Pecans with brown butter & sage, p62; Spinach tapenade with halloumi, p84; Baked pumpkin, beet & cheese, p108; Coffee granita & vanilla yogurt, p110.

Reduced cognitive ability

Coffee, kale, chard, sage, legumes, black grapes, nuts, yeast, cantaloupe, cherries, dark chocolate, red wine, eggs, apples, green tea, eggplant, chiles, carrots, dairy, brown rice, spinach, mackerel, oats, wild salmon, berries, Brussels sprouts, cherries, avocados

Recipes include:
Scrambled eggs & smoked salmon, p50; Parsnip, sage & chest-nut soup, p89; Lamb with kale & spicy tomato salsa, p102; Coffee & walnut cake, p114.

Slow circulation

Avocados, beets, blueberries, black grapes, watermelon, dark chocolate, goji berries, sunflower seeds, pomegranate, pecans, flax seeds, spinach, Brussels sprouts, wild salmon, walnuts, celery, kale, bananas, almonds, garlic, oranges, oats, ginger, prunes, sage, bell peppers, chiles, onions, legumes

Recipes include:
Muesli with honey & grapes, p47; Parsnip & beet chips, p58; Smoked duck & clementine salad, p74; Bean burgers with pecan coleslaw, p109.

Stress

Avocados, broccoli, brown rice, dark chocolate, eggs, apples, chiles, oats, pecans, pumpkin and flax seeds, wild salmon, asparagus, kiwifruit, blue- and strawberries, beef, legumes, walnuts, seaweed, mango, turkey, spinach, tuna, almonds, dairy, sweet potatoes, olives, oranges, chicken

Recipes include:
Blueberry & avocado smoothie, p38; Smoked salmon & edamame cups, p52; Cremini mushroom pilaf, p103; Chocolate-dipped strawberries, p116.

Disturbed sleep

Avocados, chard, kale, kidney beans, live yogurt, brown rice, seafood, wild salmon, pecans, spinach, walnuts, flax seeds, oats, popcorn, peanuts, black grapes, soybeans, seeds, honey, almonds, bananas, papaya, mushrooms, turkey

Recipes include:
Apricot & prune granola, p46; Cocoa, orange & pecan oat bars, p66; Spicy chard & bean soup, p88; Quail with ginger & grapes, p98.

Anxiety

Eggs, chiles, live yogurt, oats, spinach, wild salmon, beets, flax seeds, nuts, dark chocolate, peaches, almonds, soybeans and fava beans, bananas, melon, lettuce, acai berries, raspberries, whole grains, brewer's yeast, quinoa, cabbage

Recipes include:
Apple cinnamon porridge, p40; Apple & walnut squares, p44; Bell pepper, feta & egg tagine, p92; Spicy chicken with lemon rice, p94.

Dementia

Eggs, Granny Smith apples, chiles, kale, kidney beans, black grapes, mackerel, oats, pecans, sage, spinach, flax seeds, strawberries, dark chocolate, walnuts, wild salmon, avocados, beets, blueberries, coffee

Recipes include:
Scrambled egg enchiladas, p48; Balsamic avocado & strawberries, p54; Walnut-crusted salmon, p90; Apple, maple & pecan whips, p124.

Poor neurotransmitter health

Eggs, chiles, kale, live yogurt, oats, pecans, sage, chard, cheese, spinach, avocados, almonds, brown rice, coffee, black grapes, dark chocolate, walnuts, quinoa, bananas, fava beans, oily fish, oranges, flax, sesame, and pumpkin seeds

Recipes include:
Fried eggs with sage, p51; Butternut, chard & herb tart, p82; Ginger & lime mackerel, p95; Chocolate avocado pudding, p118.

High levels of toxicity

Oats, Granny Smith apples, kale, kidney beans, spinach, flax seeds, strawberries, avocados, beets, brown rice, broccoli, black grapes, chard, blueberries, olive oil, artichokes, turmeric, asparagus, lemons, cabbage, seaweed, garlic, watercress ginger, grapefruit, green tea

Recipes include:
Strawberry & grape smoothie, p36; Beet & horseradish hummus, p60; Apple, avocado & spinach salad, p76; Spaghetti with kale & tomatoes, p106.

Fluctuating blood sugar

Brown rice, onions, black grapes, dark chocolate, eggs, flax and sunflower seeds, tuna, Granny Smith apples, cinnamon, kale, watermelon, live yogurt, beets, avocados, turmeric, mackerel, oats, nuts, wild salmon, millet, black-, blue- and raspberries, quinoa, figs, legumes, sweet potatoes, grapefruit

Recipes include:
Muesli with honey & grapes, p47; Kidney bean dip & flax crackers, p57; Rice, pecan & cranberry salad, p72; Crispy salmon ramen, p96.

PUTTING IT ALL TOGETHER

Meal Planner	Monday	Tuesday	Wednesday
Breakfast	Apricot & prune granola, p46	Blueberry & avocado smoothie, p38	Apple & walnut squares, p44
Morning snack	Balsamic avocado & strawberries, p54	Cocoa, orange & pecan oat bars, p66	Parsnip & beet chips, p58
Lunch	Smoked haddock & kale soup, p86	Apple, avocado & spinach salad, p76	Asparagus with smoked salmon, p85
Afternoon snack	Blueberry & flax seed bread, p64	Kidney bean dip & flax crackers, p57	Chewy oat & raisin bars, p71
Dinner	Spaghetti with kale & tomatoes, p106	Ginger & lime mackerel, p95	Bean burgers with pecan coleslaw, p109
Dessert	Coffee granita & vanilla yogurt, p110	Orange & chocolate tart, p115	Frozen berry yogurt, p123

WEEK 1

Thursday

Whole-wheat blueberry pancakes, p39

Pecans with brown butter & sage, p62

Spicy chard & bean soup, p88

Beet & horseradish hummus, p60

Walnut-crusted salmon, p90

Apple, maple & pecan whips, p124

Friday

Strawberry & grape smoothie, p36

Mackerel pâté & pita bites, p63

Rice, pecan & cranberry salad, p72

Herbed apple compote, p70

Baked pumpkin, beets & cheese p108

Cinnamon-baked apples, p119

Saturday

Scrambled egg enchiladas, p48

Balsamic avocado & strawberries, p54

Falafels with beet salad, p77

Smoked salmon & edamame cups, p52

Espresso & chili pork tenderloin, p100

Chocolate avocado pudding, p118

Sunday

Spiced French fruit bread with berry yogurt, p42

Apple & nutmeg smoothie, p68

Spinach tapenade with pan-fried cheese, p84

Spicy mixed bean salsa, p56

Crispy salmon ramen, p96

Fruit parcels & pistachio yogurt, p120

Meal Planner	Monday	Tuesday	Wednesday
Breakfast	Muesli with honey & grapes, p47	Fried eggs with sage, p51	Apple cinnamon porridge, p40
Morning snack	Granny Smith apple and a small chunk of cheese	Parsnip & beet chips, p58	Kidney bean dip & flax crackers, p57
Lunch	Parsnip, sage & chestnut soup, p89	Smoked duck & clementine salad, p74	Beet & mackerel lentils, p78
Afternoon snack	Cocoa, orange & pecan oat bars, p66	Blueberry & flax seed bread, p64	Pecans with brown butter & sage, p62
Dinner	Spicy chicken with lemon rice, p94	Fragrant vegetarian chili, p104	Bell pepper, feta & egg tagine, p92
Dessert	Coffee desserts, p112	Chocolate-dipped strawberries, p116	Coffee & walnut cake, p114

WEEK 2

Thursday

Blueberry
& avocado
smoothie, p38

Cocoa, orange &
pecan oat bars, p66

Butternut, chard
& herb tart, p82

Spicy mixed
bean salsa, p56

Walnut-crusted
salmon, p90

Cinnamon-baked
apples, p119

Friday

Apple & walnut
squares, p44

Balsamic avocado
& strawberries, p54

Asparagus
with smoked
salmon, p85

Beet & horseradish
hummus, p60

Cremini mushroom
pilaf, p103

Blueberry & date
mousse, p122

Saturday

Whole-wheat
blueberry
pancakes, p39

Herbed apple
compote, p70

Rice, pecan &
cranberry salad, p72

Mackerel pâté & pita
bites, p63

Quail with ginger
& grapes, p98

Coffee granita &
vanilla yogurt, p110

Sunday

Scrambled
eggs & smoked
salmon, p50

Apple & nutmeg
smoothie, p68

Cheese roulade
with spinach, p80

Pecans with brown
butter & sage, p62

Lamb with kale
& spicy tomato
salsa, p102

Frozen berry
yogurt, p123

SMART
RECIPES

STRAWBERRY & GRAPE SMOOTHIE

Fresh, fruity, and absolutely delicious, this nourishing smoothie is ideal for a quick, energy-boosting breakfast or a filling snack.

Preparation time: 10 minutes
Serves 4
....

2 cups fresh or frozen
strawberries, hulled
3 cups **black grapes**
1 cup **light coconut milk**
8 **ice cubes**

Place the ingredients in a blender (including any seeds in the black grapes) and blend until smooth. Serve chilled.
....

BLUEBERRY & AVOCADO SMOOTHIE

This very smooth smoothie is not only incredibly filling but full of nutrients to keep your brain working at optimum levels.

Preparation time: 10 minutes
Serves 4

2 cups fresh or frozen **blueberries**
2 **avocados**, peeled, seeded, and chopped
1¼ cups **almond milk**
½ cup pressed **apple juice**
2 tablespoons **honey**

Place all the ingredients in a liquidizer and blend until smooth. Serve chilled.

WHOLE-WHEAT BLUEBERRY PANCAKES

The whole family will be clamoring for these sensational pancakes, which are good for the digestive system as well as the brain.

Preparation time: 5 minutes
Cooking time: 25 minutes
Serves 4
....

1¼ cups **wholewheat flour**
½ cup **all-purpose flour**
1 teaspoon **baking powder**
1¼ cups **milk**
1 **egg**, beaten
2 tablespoons liquid **honey**, plus extra to serve
1 cup **blueberries**, plus extra to decorate
2 tablespoons **coconut oil**
1 tablespoon **lemon curd**
½ cup **plain live yogurt**

Sift the flours and baking powder into a large bowl, and then make a well in the center. Mix the milk, egg, and honey in a measuring jug, then pour into the dry ingredients and beat to combine well. Stir in most of the blueberries, reserving a few for decoration.

....

Heat the coconut oil in a large skillet over high heat. Ladle 2 tablespoons of the batter into the pan to make 1 pancake. Repeat to make 3 more. Cook them for 4 to 5 minutes, or until golden underneath. Flip them over and cook on the other side for a further 2 to 3 minutes. Keep the cooked pancakes warm in the oven while you make 2 more batches in the same way.

....

Mix the lemon curd and yogurt in a small bowl. Serve the pancakes with the yogurt alongside, scattered with the remaining blueberries, and drizzled with a little extra honey.

....

APPLE CINNAMON PORRIDGE

With all the brain-supporting nutrients of pecans and apples, this is a seriously smart breakfast.

Preparation time: 5 minutes
Cooking time: 10 minutes
Serves 4

....

½ cup **pecans**
2 cups **water**
2 cups **soymilk**
1 tablespoon **dark brown sugar**
2 teaspoons **ground cinnamon**
1 teaspoon grated **nutmeg**
1½ cups **rolled oats**
2 **Granny Smith apples**, cored and diced
3 tablespoons **maple syrup**

Spread the pecans out on a baking pan and place in a preheated oven, at 300°F, for about 8 minutes, or until lightly toasted.

....

Meanwhile, put the water, soymilk, sugar, and spices in a large saucepan and bring to a boil. Reduce the heat, stir in the oats and apples, and simmer for about 5 minutes, or until all of the liquid has been absorbed and the oats are tender.

....

Remove from the heat and divide among 4 serving bowls or glasses. Top with the toasted pecans and drizzle with the maple syrup to serve.

....

SPICED FRENCH FRUIT BREAD WITH BERRY YOGURT

Berries provide a powerful dose of antioxidants, while the egg provides energy to keep you going through the morning.

Preparation time: 5 minutes
Cooking time: 10 minutes
Serves 4
....

2 **eggs**
2 tablespoons **granulated sugar**
½ teaspoon **ground cinnamon**
¼ cup **milk**
2 tablespoons **butter**
4 slices of **fruit bread**
1 cup mixed **berries**, divided
½ cup **Greek yogurt**
4 teaspoons **honey**, to serve

Beat the eggs in a bowl with the sugar, cinnamon, and milk. Heat the butter in a large, heavy skillet. Dip the fruit-bread slices, 2 at a time, into the egg mixture, covering both sides. Then put the dipped bread into the hot skillet and cook for 1 to 2 minutes on each side, until golden. Repeat with the remaining fruit bread.
....

Mix half of the berries into the yogurt.
....

Serve the warm fruit-bread slices with spoonfuls of the fruit yogurt on top, sprinkled with the remaining berries, and drizzled with the honey.
....

APPLE & WALNUT SQUARES

These chewy, nutty squares are packed with the nutrients that stabilize blood-sugar levels, lift your mood, and help you focus.

Preparation time: 10 minutes
Cooking time: 30 minutes
Makes 12
....

1⅓ sticks (⅔ cup) **butter**, softened, plus extra for greasing
1 cup **light brown sugar**
¾ cup **rolled oats**
2 **eggs**, lightly beaten
1⅔ cups **all-purpose flour,** sifted with 1⅔ teaspoons **baking powder**
3 **Granny Smith apples**, cored and minced
1 teaspoon **ground cinnamon**
1 teaspoon **ground ginger**
¾ cup coarsely chopped **walnut pieces**

Put the butter and sugar in a large bowl and beat until light and fluffy. Add the oats and eggs and the sifted flour and baking powder mixture. Beat again until smooth. Fold in the apples, cinnamon, ginger, and walnuts and stir until just mixed.

....

Spread the mixture over the bottom of a greased 12 x 9-inch baking pan and place in a preheated oven, at 350°F, for 30 minutes or until golden and risen. Let cool before cutting into 12 squares or bars. The squares can be stored in an airtight container for up to 4 days and can be frozen.

....

APRICOT & PRUNE GRANOLA

A chewy, crunchy, and filling breakfast brimming with B vitamins, fiber, and omega-3s to get those brain cells firing.

Preparation time: 5 minutes
Cooking time: 5 minutes
Serves 4

½ cup whole **hazelnuts**
¾ cup rolled **oats**
2 cups Bran Flakes, All-Bran,
or similar **bran-based breakfast cereal**
2 tablespoons **sunflower** or
mixed **seeds** (optional)
½ cup sliced **dried apricots**
5 **dried prunes**, chopped

To serve
milk
honey
sliced **banana** or **apple** (optional)

Put the hazelnuts in a small, dry skillet and heat gently for 4 to 5 minutes, shaking the skillet occasionally, until lightly toasted.

Transfer into the bowl of a mortar, crush lightly with a pestle, and set aside to cool.

Meanwhile, combine the oats, bran cereal, seeds, and dried fruits. Add the hazelnuts, then divide among 4 serving bowls and serve immediately with milk and honey and sliced banana or apple, if desired. Alternatively, double the recipe and store for up to a week in an airtight container.

MUESLI WITH HONEY & GRAPES

This delicious Bircher muesli contains great levels of fiber, omega oils, and antioxidants to set you up for the day.

Preparation time: 5 minutes, plus soaking
Serves 4

....

1¼ cups **steel-cut oats**
⅔ cup **plain live yogurt**
1 cup **almond milk**
1 tablespoon chopped **dates**
3 tablespoons **dried blueberries**
3 tablespoons **golden raisins**
2 tablespoons **ground flax seeds**
1 teaspoon **ground cinnamon**
1 tablespoon **honey**, plus extra to serve
2 handfuls of **black grapes**, halved

Put all the ingredients, except for the grapes, in a large bowl and mix well. Cover and let stand in the refrigerator overnight to soak.

....

When ready to serve, stir in the grapes, divide among 4 bowls, and drizzle with a little extra honey.

....

SCRAMBLED EGG ENCHILADAS

Make these as spicy as you like, because the chile will help increase concentration and provide you with a hefty dose of multivitamins for memory.

Preparation time: 15 minutes
Cooking time: 25 minutes
Serves 4

3 tablespoons **olive oil**
1 small **red onion**, chopped
1 **garlic clove**, crushed
1 small **red bell pepper**, cored, seeded, and cut into strips
1 **red chile**, cored, seeded, and chopped
½ teaspoon **smoked paprika**
pinch of **ground coriander**
salt and **black pepper**
2 tablespoons **butter**
4 **eggs**, beaten
4 soft flour **tortillas**
2 handfuls of **baby spinach leaves**
¾ cup shredded **cheddar cheese**
2 **tomatoes**, chopped

Heat the oil in a small skillet, add the onion, garlic, red bell pepper, and chile and cook over low heat, stirring occasionally, for 10 minutes or until soft and tender.

Stir in the paprika and coriander, season with salt and black pepper, and cook for another 2 minutes.

Melt the butter in a separate small saucepan (preferably nonstick). Season the eggs with salt and black pepper and pour into the pan. Cook over low heat, stirring, until the egg is softly set and scrambled, and then remove from the heat.

Lay the tortillas out on a board, arrange the spinach leaves on top, then spoon the onion mixture and the scrambled eggs over the spinach. Fold the tortillas into triangles to enclose the filling and place in a baking dish. Sprinkle with the cheese and chopped tomatoes and bake in a preheated oven, at 400°F, for 10 minutes, until the cheese is melted and bubbling.

SCRAMBLED EGGS & SMOKED SALMON

This hearty breakfast is teeming with omega-3 oils, antioxidants, healthy fats, and a wealth of other nutrients, making it perfect for a demanding day.

Preparation time: 10 minutes
Cooking time: 10 minutes
Serves 4

3 tablespoons snipped **chives**, plus extra to garnish
2 tablespoons **plain live yogurt**
6 large **eggs**
sea salt and **black pepper**
1 tablespoon **butter**
1 **avocado**, peeled, seeded, and coarsely chopped
1 teaspoon **lemon juice**
4 slices of **whole-wheat toast**
3½ oz **smoked wild salmon**

Put the chives, yogurt, and eggs in a large bowl, season to taste, and beat until fluffy. Meanwhile, melt the butter in a saucepan (preferably nonstick) over low heat and add the egg mixture. Season to taste and cook, stirring, until softly set and scrambled. Remove from the heat.

Place the avocado and lemon juice in a small bowl, season to taste, and mash until smooth. Spread the mixture on the toast, top with the scrambled eggs, and arrange the smoked salmon over the top. Grind a little black pepper on the salmon, garnish with a few chives, and serve immediately.

FRIED EGGS WITH SAGE

A quick and easy breakfast to lift mood and energy levels, and get your brain on track for the day ahead.

Preparation time: 5 minutes
Cooking time: 10 minutes
Serves 4

....

1 tablespoon **olive oil**
small handful of **sage** leaves
1½ cups **mushrooms**, sliced
4 large **eggs**
sea salt and **black pepper**
whole-wheat toast, to serve

Heat the olive oil in a large skillet over medium heat and add the sage leaves. When they begin to lose color and become crisp at the edges, remove from the skillet and drain on paper towels.

Add the mushrooms to the skillet and cook for about 3 to 5 minutes or until just tender. Remove them from the skillet and set aside. Increase the heat and fry the eggs in the skillet until the whites are set.

Divide the mushrooms among 4 plates, place a fried egg on top of each portion, and then sprinkle with the toasted sage leaves. Season to taste and serve with whole-wheat toast.

SMOKED SALMON & EDAMAME CUPS

The omega-3-rich salmon and slivers of chile in these delectable lettuce cups make them a luxury brain snack par excellence.

Preparation time: 10 minutes
Cooking time: 2 minutes
Serves 4
....

2 cups frozen **edamame** (soybeans)
7 oz **smoked wild salmon**, thinly sliced
¼ **cucumber**, seeded and cut into matchsticks
1 **red chile**, seeded and sliced
2 tablespoons **light soy sauce**
2 tablespoons coarsely chopped **cilantro** leaves (optional)
3 to 4 **Little Gem lettuces**, leaves separated
2 teaspoons flax seeds

Cook the edamame in a large saucepan of salted, boiling water for 2 to 3 minutes, or according to the package directions, until just tender. Drain and cool under cold running water.
....

Meanwhile, combine the salmon, cucumber, chile, soy sauce, and cilantro in a bowl. Add the beans and toss gently to combine.
....

Spoon the bean mixture into individual lettuce leaves and sprinkle with the flax seeds. Serve immediately.
....

BALSAMIC AVOCADO & STRAWBERRIES

This super-quick-to-make snack will increase alertness and energy, while helping relieve symptoms of stress, which can affect concentration.

Preparation time: 5 minutes
Serves 4

....

1 cup **strawberries**, hulled
1 tablespoon **balsamic vinegar**
1 teaspoon **olive oil**
sea salt
2 **avocados**, peeled, seeded, and cut into chunks
2 tablespoons shredded **mint** leaves

Put the hulled strawberries in a mixing bowl. Drizzle with the vinegar and oil and season with salt to taste. Gently stir in the chopped avocado, and then use a slotted spoon to divide among 4 plates. Sprinkle with the mint leaves before serving.

....

Leftovers can be stored in the vinegar and oil marinade, sealed in an airtight container in the refrigerator for up to 2 days.

....

SPICY MIXED BEAN SALSA

This tasty salsa works wonders as an instant pick-me-up and will help you focus your brain.

Preparation time: 15 minutes
Serves 4
....

½ cup canned **kidney beans**, rinsed and drained
½ cup canned **black beans**, rinsed and drained
½ cup canned **pinto beans**, rinsed and drained
1 **red bell pepper**, cored, seeded, and chopped
1 **red onion**, diced
1 **red chile**, seeded and diced
1 **avocado**, peeled, seeded, and cut into chunks
1 teaspoon **ground cumin**
1 tablespoon **olive oil**
finely grated zest and juice of 1 **lemon**
handful of fresh **cilantro**, chopped
sea salt and **black pepper**
whole-wheat pita bread or **unsalted tortilla chips**, to serve

Put all the salsa ingredients in a large bowl, season to taste, and stir to combine. Serve immediately with warmed pita bread or unsalted tortilla chips.
....

Leftover salsa can be stored in an airtight container in the refrigerator for up to 2 days.
....

KIDNEY BEAN DIP & FLAX CRACKERS

This spicy dip is easy to make, and can be served with flax seed crackers, on whole-wheat toast, or as a dip for crudités.

Preparation time: 20 minutes, plus cooling
Cooking time: 20 to 30 minutes
Serves 4

....

1 tablespoon **olive oil**
1 small **onion**, diced
2 **garlic cloves**, chopped
½ small **chile**, seeded and minced
1 teaspoon **ground cumin**
1⅓ cups quartered **cherry tomatoes**
1 (14 oz) can **kidney beans**, rinsed and drained
2 tablespoons **plain Greek yogurt**
sea salt and **black pepper**

For the crackers
2¾ cups **ground flax seeds**
½ teaspoon **salt**
½ teaspoon **black pepper**
1 **garlic clove**, finely chopped
1 teaspoon **onion powder**
1 cup **water**

For the crackers, put the ground flax seeds in a bowl with the salt, pepper, garlic, and onion powder. Mix well, then slowly add the water, a little at a time, until the mixture forms a stiff dough.

Spread the mixture evenly on the bottom of a greased 12 x 9-inch baking pan and smooth the surface with a metal spatula. Use a sharp knife and a ruler to score the dough into 24 even squares.

Place in a preheated oven, at 350°F, for 20 to 30 minutes or until crisp and golden. Let cool, and then snap the crackers apart along the scored lines.

Meanwhile, make the dip. Heat the oil in a small skillet over medium–low heat, add the onion, garlic, and chile and cook for about 3 minutes, stirring from time to time. Add the cumin, tomatoes, and beans and cook for 2 to 3 minutes more. Season to taste, and then transfer to a food processor. Add the yogurt and blend until smooth. Serve the dip with the crackers.

Any leftover crackers can be stored in an airtight container for up to a week.

PARSNIP & BEET CHIPS

You can use any root vegetables for your chips, but remember that beets are the ones with plenty of iron to help transport oxygenated blood to the brain.

Preparation time: 10 minutes
Cooking time: 10 minutes
Serves 4
....

sunflower or vegetable oil, for deep-frying
2 parsnips, peeled, halved, and thinly sliced lengthwise
2 to 3 raw beets, peeled and thinly sliced
salt and black pepper

For the dukkah spice mix
1 tablespoon **hazelnuts**
1 tablespoon **sesame seeds**
2 teaspoons **cumin seeds**
2 teaspoons **coriander seeds**
2 teaspoons **dried mint**

To make the spice mix, dry-fry the nuts and seeds in a small, heavy skillet over medium heat for 2 to 3 minutes, or until they emit a nutty aroma. Then use a mortar and pestle and pound the nuts and seeds to a coarse powder, or add to a spice grinder and grind to a fine powder. Stir in the dried mint and season well. Set aside.

....

In a deep saucepan, heat enough oil for deep-frying. When it reaches 350°F to 375°F, or when a cube of bread browns in the hot oil in 30 seconds, the oil is ready. Deep-fry the parsnips in batches until lightly browned. Remove with a slotted spoon and drain on paper towels. When they are all cooked, reduce the heat under the oil and transfer all of the parsnips to a bowl while still hot. Sprinkle with half of the spice mix, toss to coat, and set aside.

....

The beet slices burn easily so cook them once the oil has cooled a little. Deep-fry the beets in batches. Remove and drain as above. Then transfer to a bowl, sprinkle with the remaining spice mix, and toss to coat. Serve the parsnip and beet chips separately or mixed together.

....

BEET & HORSERADISH HUMMUS

The deep-red color of this yummy hummus comes from the betalain antioxidants, which help prevent memory loss.

Preparation time: 10 minutes
Serves 4
....

3½ cups coarsely diced **cooked beets**
2 tablespoons **horseradish sauce**
1 (45 oz) can **chickpeas**, rinsed
and drained
½ teaspoon **ground cumin**
2 tablespoons **olive oil**
1 teaspoon **lemon juice**
salt and **black pepper**
snipped **chives**, to garnish

To serve
plain live yogurt
whole-wheat pita bread,
toasted and cut into strips

Put the diced beets into a food processor along with the horseradish sauce, chickpeas, cumin, olive oil, lemon juice, and a generous pinch of salt and black pepper. Blend until almost smooth.
....

Spoon into bowls and top with a spoonful of yogurt. Garnish with the snipped chives and serve with strips of pita bread.
....

PECANS WITH BROWN BUTTER & SAGE

This somewhat decadent snack will almost instantly have a positive effect on your blood sugar, mood, and concentration.

Preparation time: 5 minutes
Cooking time: 20 minutes
Serves 8

....

3 tablespoons **butter**
1 teaspoon **sea salt**
2 tablespoons finely sliced **sage** leaves, divided
2½ cups whole **pecans**

Melt the butter in a large, heavy saucepan over medium heat. Cook for 2 to 3 minutes, or until it starts to brown. Add the salt and half the sage and cook for a further minute. Remove from the heat. Add the pecans and stir to coat.

....

Arrange the pecans in a single layer on a nonstick cookie sheet and then place in a preheated oven, at 350°F, for 10 minutes, or until fragrant and lightly toasted. Sprinkle with the remaining sage and cook for an additional 2 minutes.

....

Remove the nuts from the oven and let cool on the cookie sheet. When cool, add to a bowl and toss gently to serve.

....

Leftover nuts can be stored in an airtight container in the refrigerator for up to 1 week.

....

MACKEREL PÂTÉ & PITA BITES

This easy-to-make pâté is bursting with omega-3 oils, vitamins, and minerals to give your brain a boost when you need it most.

Preparation time: 10 minutes
Serves 4 to 6

13 oz **smoked mackerel**,
skin and bones removed
1 cup **low-fat crème fraîche**
finely grated zest and juice of 1 **lemon**
1 teaspoon chopped **dill**
1 tablespoon chopped **parsley**
black pepper
whole-wheat pita bread, toasted
and cut into strips, to serve

Put the pâté ingredients in a food processor. Season with freshly ground black pepper, and blend until smooth. Serve the pâté with the toasted pita bread strips.

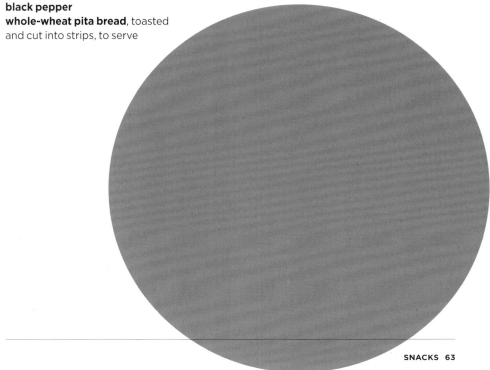

BLUEBERRY & FLAX SEED BREAD

This is a fabulous nutrient- and fiber-rich bread to soothe, balance, and return your brain to peak form.

Preparation time: 10 minutes, plus cooling
Cooking time: 45 to 55 minutes
Makes 10 slices

oil, for greasing
⅓ cup **sunflower oil**
⅓ cup **lemon juice**
1¼ cups **soft brown sugar**
2 teaspoons **vanilla extract**
⅔ cup **soymilk**
1 cup **ground flax seeds**
2½ cups **whole-wheat flour**
2 teaspoons **baking powder**
½ tsp **baking soda**
1⅔ cups fresh or frozen **blueberries**

Lightly grease a large loaf pan.

Add the sunflower oil, lemon juice, sugar, vanilla, and soymilk to a large mixing bowl, and then stir in the ground flax seeds. Sift in the flour, baking powder, and baking soda and stir to combine.

Gently fold the blueberries into the batter, and then pour it into the prepared loaf pan. Place in a preheated oven, at 350°F, and bake for 45 to 55 minutes or until risen and golden brown and a skewer inserted in the center comes out clean. Turn out onto a wire rack. Once cool, serve in slices.

COCOA, ORANGE & PECAN OAT BARS

Pecans are truly miraculous nuts with minerals, omega-3s, and vitamin E, to support the brain; reach for one of these when your IQ needs a boost.

Preparation time: 5 minutes, plus cooling
Cooking time: 25 minutes
Makes 12

2½ tablespoons **dark brown sugar** ½ cup **coconut oil**, plus extra for greasing
¼ cup **molasses**
1 tablespoon **agave syrup**
2¾ cups rolled **oats**
½ cup coarsely chopped **pecans**
½ cup **cocoa nibs**
finely grated zest of 1 **orange**

Grease a 7-inch square baking pan.

In a large saucepan, melt together the sugar, coconut oil, molasses, and agave syrup until the sugar has dissolved.

Add the remaining ingredients and stir to combine. Pour the mixture into the greased pan and level off the top.

Bake the oat bars in a preheated oven, at 350°F, for 18 to 20 minutes. Remove from the oven and cut into 12 squares. Let cool in the pan.

APPLE & NUTMEG SMOOTHIE

The fiber, antioxidants, and calcium in this satisfying smoothie will help when your concentration and blood sugar have dipped.

Preparation time: 5 minutes
Serves 4

3 **Granny Smith apples**, cored and chopped
1 cup pressed **apple juice**
1 cup **plain Greek yogurt**
8 **ice cubes**
½ teaspoon **ground cinnamon**
1 teaspoon grated **nutmeg**
½ teaspoon **ground ginger**

Put all of the ingredients in a blender and blend until smooth. Serve chilled.

HERBED APPLE COMPOTE

This chunky, warming compote will boost memory, blood sugar, and concentration and is perfect for a quick snack.

Preparation time: 10 minutes
Cooking time: 25 to 30 minutes
Serves 4
....

8 **Granny Smith apples**,
cored and cut into chunks
2 **Pink Lady apples**,
cored and cut into chunks
3 **rosemary** leaves
½ cup **water**
2 tablespoons **maple syrup**
1 teaspoon **ground cinnamon**
1 tablespoon chopped **sage**

Put the apples, rosemary, and water in a large, heavy saucepan and bring to a boil. Reduce the heat, cover, and simmer for 15 to 20 minutes, or until the apples are just starting to break down into the liquid.

Place half of the mixture in a blender and blend until smooth. Return this to the pan and add the maple syrup, cinnamon, and sage. Give it a good stir and cook for a further 2 to 3 minutes. Serve warm or cold.

CHEWY OAT & RAISIN BARS

Simple to make and easy to transport, these yummy bars are useful brain food when you are on the move.

Preparation time: 5 minutes
Cooking time: 20 minutes
Makes 16

....

oil, for greasing
1¾ sticks (¼ cup plus 3 tablespoons) **butter**
⅓ cup **honey**
⅔ cup sweetened **condensed milk**
½ cup **turbinado sugar**
3½ cups rolled **oats**
½ cup **raisins**
⅔ cup **all-purpose flour** sifted with
⅔ teaspoon **baking powder**

Grease with oil a 1½-inch deep, 10-inch square cake pan. Line the bottom with nonstick parchment paper and set aside.

Add the butter, corn syrup, milk, and sugar to a large saucepan set over medium-low heat. Stir until the sugar dissolves, and then remove from the heat. Stir in the rolled oats and the raisins, along with the sifted flour and baking powder and stir well to combine.

Scrape the batter into the prepared pan and bake in a preheated oven, at 350°F, for 15 to 18 minutes or until pale golden.

Remove from the oven and let cool in the pan for 2 to 3 minutes before marking out and cutting about 16 squares or bars. Let stand for another 5 minutes, or until cool and firm enough to handle. Then transfer the bars to a wire rack to cool completely.

These bars will keep for up to 1 week in an airtight container.

RICE, PECAN & CRANBERRY SALAD

This simple salad will stabilize blood sugar, focus the mind, and aid relaxation. It can be served warm or cold.

Preparation time: 20 minutes
Cooking time: 25 minutes
Serves 4
....

1 cup **brown rice**
3 oz **kale**
¾ cup **pecans**, lightly toasted
2 **scallions**, minced
½ cup **dried cranberries**
2 teaspoons **thyme** leaves, plus extra to garnish
finely grated zest and juice of 2 **oranges**
1 tablespoon **balsamic vinegar**
2 tablespoons **honey**
1 teaspoon **sea salt**
1 teaspoon **black pepper**
2 tablespoons **olive oil**
3½ oz **feta cheese**, cubed

Cook the rice in a saucepan of lightly salted boiling water, according to the package instructions, until tender. Pour the cooked rice into a strainer, rinse under cold running water, and let it drain. Steam the kale in a steamer over a saucepan of simmering water until just tender; then slice finely, and let cool.
....

Put the rice in a large bowl with the pecans, scallions, cranberries, kale, and thyme and mix together well. Put the orange juice and zest, vinegar, honey, sea salt, pepper, and oil in a small bowl and whisk to combine. Pour the dressing evenly over the rice mixture and toss together. If it's a little dry, add more orange juice. Add the feta cheese cubes and toss the salad gently before sprinkling with extra thyme to serve.
....

SMOKED DUCK & CLEMENTINE SALAD

The bright colors show that this salad is rich in antioxidants, while the walnuts provide omega-3 oils and vitamin E for brain health.

Preparation time: 10 minutes
Serves 4
....

2 **clementines**
½ bunch of **watercress**, plus a handful of extra leaves, to garnish
½ cup **walnuts**, lightly crushed
8 oz **smoked duck breast**, sliced
pomegranate seeds, to garnish (optional)

Dressing
2 tablespoons **walnut oil**
2 teaspoons **raspberry vinegar**
salt and **black pepper**

Cut away the clementines' peel and pith. Cut the flesh into segments, discarding the membrane, but reserving the juice in a small bowl.
....

Divide the watercress among 4 plates and sprinkle with the clementine segments and the walnut pieces. Top the salad with the smoked duck slices and garnish with the watercress leaves and pomegranate seeds, if using.
....

For the dressing, whisk the oil and vinegar into the reserved clementine juice and season to taste. Drizzle the dressing over each portion and serve.
....

APPLE, AVOCADO & SPINACH SALAD

This salad works on all levels to encourage brain health. If stress is bogging you down, you should expect a relief from symptoms after this salad lunch.

Preparation time: 15 minutes
Serves 4

7 oz **baby spinach**
2 **Granny Smith apples**,
cored and cut into chunks
2 **avocados**, peeled,
seeded, and cut into chunks
½ **red onion**, thinly sliced
1 small **carrot**, grated
1 small raw **beet**, grated
1 **celery** stalk, chopped
¾ cup **walnut pieces**, lightly toasted
handful of **basil**, torn

Dressing
3 tablespoons **plain live yogurt**
1 **garlic clove**, crushed
1 large **red chile**, seeded and minced
finely grated zest and juice of ½ **lemon**
1½ tablespoons **honey**
2 tablespoons **olive oil**
sea salt and **black pepper**

Arrange all the salad ingredients in a large salad bowl and toss to combine.

Put all the dressing ingredients in a small bowl or pitcher, season to taste, and whisk to combine. Pour the dressing evenly over the salad, toss to coat, and serve.

FALAFELS WITH BEET SALAD

You can see from the glorious colors of this dish that it is packed with nutrients, and the fresh, light flavors will make it a favorite.

Preparation time: 15 minutes
Cooking time: 10 minutes
Serves 2

1 (15 oz) can **chickpeas**, rinsed and drained
½ small **red onion**, coarsely chopped
1 **garlic clove**, chopped
½ **red chile**, seeded
1 teaspoon **ground cumin**
1 teaspoon **ground coriander**
handful of **flat-leaf parsley**
salt and **black pepper**
2 tablespoons **olive oil**

Beet salad
1 **carrot**, shredded
1 raw **beet**, shredded
2 cups **baby spinach**
1 tablespoon **lemon juice**
2 tablespoons **olive oil**

Mint yogurt
⅔ cup **plain Greek yogurt**
1 tablespoon chopped **mint** leaves
½ **garlic clove**, crushed

To make the falafels, add the chickpeas, onion, garlic, chile, cumin, coriander, and parsley to a food processor. Season, then blend to make a coarse paste. Shape the mixture into 8 patties and arrange them on a baking sheet. Place in the fridge to get firm.

Meanwhile, make the salad. Put the carrot, beet, and spinach in a bowl. Season, add the lemon juice and oil, and toss to coat.

Now make the mint yogurt. Mix together all the ingredients and season with a little salt.

Remove the falafels from the refrigerator. Heat the oil in a skillet over medium heat, add the falafels, and fry for 4 to 5 minutes on each side or until golden. Serve with the beet salad and mint yogurt.

BEET & MACKEREL LENTILS

Equally delicious whether served warm from the stove or cold from a lunchbox, this is a filling, omega-rich salad for days when you need to be at your best.

Preparation time: 5 minutes, plus cooling
Cooking time: 18 minutes
Serves 4
················

1 cup **dried green lentils**
3 tablespoons **olive oil**
2 **red onions**, finely sliced
½ cup **balsamic vinegar**
2 cups rinsed and diced
cooked beets
2 (3¾ oz) cans **mackerel**,
drained and flaked
7 oz firm **goat cheese**,
crumbled or diced
snipped **chives**, to garnish (optional)

Cook the dried lentils in a large saucepan of lightly salted boiling water for about 15 to 18 minutes or until tender but still holding their shape. Drain and set aside.

Meanwhile, heat the oil in a large skillet over low heat. Add the onion and cook gently for 12 to 15 minutes or until soft and lightly browned. Pour the balsamic vinegar evenly over the red onion and simmer gently for 2 to 3 minutes or until the vinegar begins to turn slightly syrupy.

Remove from the heat and gently stir the lentils into the onion, along with the diced beets. Let cool slightly for 4 to 5 minutes, and then spoon into bowls. Sprinkle with the flaked mackerel and crumbled goat cheese. Garnish with snipped chives, if using, to serve.

CHEESE ROULADE WITH SPINACH

This is true brain food in a roll; serve slices at a working lunch to keep the ideas flowing all afternoon.

Preparation time: 15 minutes, plus cooling
Cooking time: 20 minutes
Serves 4
....

2½ tablespoons **unsalted butter**
¼ cup **gluten-free flour blend**
1 cup **milk**
pinch of **cayenne pepper**
4 extra-large **eggs**, separated
2 teaspoons **Dijon mustard**
¾ cup shredded **cheddar cheese**
½ cup finely chopped **walnuts**
1 cup **light cream cheese**
4 cups **baby spinach**
3 **scallions**, finely sliced
salt and **black pepper**

Melt the butter in a small saucepan over medium heat. Use a little of the melted butter to grease a 13 x 9-inch jellyroll pan. Line it with nonstick parchment paper and set aside.
....

Stir the flour into the melted butter in the saucepan to make a roux. Gradually whisk in the milk and continue to cook until the sauce comes to a boil and is thick and creamy. Remove from the heat, add the cayenne, and season. Stir in the egg yolks, mustard, cheddar, and the walnuts.
....

In a large grease-free bowl, whisk the egg whites with a handheld electric beater until stiff peaks form. Fold the egg whites into the cheese mixture and gently pour into the prepared pan. Bake in a preheated oven at 400°F for 10 to 12 minutes or until firm.
....

Spread out a piece of nonstick parchment paper slightly larger than the pan. Turn out the roulade onto the paper, then peel off the lining paper, and use the parchment paper to help you gently roll up the roulade. Cover with a damp cloth and let cool slightly.
....

Unroll the roulade, spread with the cream cheese, sprinkle with the spinach and scallions, then reroll. Serve warm or cold.
....

BUTTERNUT, CHARD & HERB TART

Antioxidant- and vitamin A-rich butternut squash promotes brain health. Use ready-made pastry if you are short of time.

Preparation time: 20 minutes
Cooking time: 35 minutes
Serves 4
....

½ **butternut squash**, peeled, seeded, and cubed
1 tablespoon **olive oil**
½ small **red chile**, seeded and finely chopped
sea salt and **black pepper**
14 oz **chard**, coarsely chopped
4 large **eggs**
3½ oz **pecorino cheese**
handful of **pine nuts**
handful of **basil** leaves, to garnish

Pastry
1¼ cups **all-purpose flour**
¼ cup **ground flax seeds**
½ cup **olive oil**
½ teaspoon **sea salt**
½ teaspoon **black pepper**

For the pastry, sift the flour and flax seeds into a large bowl. Make a well in the center and pour in the olive oil, salt, and pepper. Blend with a fork and then use your fingers to make a smooth dough.
....

Press the dough into the bottom and up the sides of a deep 9-inch tart pan or pie dish and trim the edges of the dough. Line with nonstick parchment paper, fill with pie weights or dried beans, and bake blind in a preheated oven, at 350°F for 10 minutes.
....

Meanwhile, toss the squash with the oil and chile, season, and spread out on a baking pan. Place in the oven for about 15 minutes, or until just tender but still holding its shape.
....

Cook the chard in a large saucepan of lightly salted boiling water for 8 to 10 minutes, or until it is tender but still has a little crunch. Drain and set aside. Put the eggs in a bowl with the pecorino and beat until well mixed.
....

Remove the pie weights or dried beans and paper from the tart crust and arrange the squash and chard in the bottom. Pour in the egg mixture and sprinkle with the pine nuts. Return to the oven for about 15 minutes or until the egg mixture has set. Serve warm or cold, sprinkled with basil leaves.
....

SPINACH TAPENADE WITH PAN-FRIED CHEESE

Rich, tasty spinach is a perfect match for the creamy chewiness of the cheese. This dish is also full of brain-stimulating vitamins.

Preparation time: 10 minutes
Cooking time: 25 minutes
Serves 4

1 (6 oz) package **baby spinach**
handful of **celery** leaves
4 tablespoons **olive oil**
2 to 3 **garlic cloves**, crushed
1 teaspoon **cumin seeds**
6 to 8 ripe **black olives**, pitted and finely chopped
large bunch of **flat-leaf parsley**, finely chopped
large bunch of **cilantro**, finely chopped
1 teaspoon Spanish **smoked paprika**
juice of ½ **lemon**
salt and **black pepper**
8 oz **Muenster** or **halloumi cheese**, sliced

Put the baby spinach and celery leaves in a steamer and cook for 10 to 15 minutes or until wilted. Refresh under cold running water, then drain well and squeeze out the excess water. Chop to a fine pulp.

Heat 2 tablespoons of the olive oil in a heavy skillet, stir in the garlic and cumin seeds, and cook until they emit a nutty aroma. Then stir in the olives, parsley, cilantro, and paprika. Add the spinach and celery leaves, season well, and cook gently for 8 to 10 minutes or until the mixture is smooth.

Meanwhile, for frying the cheese, heat the remaining oil in a separate heavy skillet, add the Muenster cheese or halloumi, and cook for 3 to 4 minutes, turning once, until golden brown and crispy. Drain on paper towels.

Transfer the spinach mixture to a bowl, add the lemon juice, and mix well. Serve warm with the fried cheese.

ASPARAGUS WITH SMOKED SALMON

All the omega goodness of salmon, eggs, and nuts, and the antioxidant power of asparagus. This is pure luxury, and you know you deserve it.

Preparation time: 10 minutes
Cooking time: 5 to 10 minutes
Serves 6

18 thin **asparagus** spears, trimmed
3 tablespoons coarsely chopped **hazelnuts**
4 teaspoons **olive oil**
juice of 1 **lime**
1 teaspoon **Dijon mustard**
salt and **black pepper**
12 **quail eggs**
8 oz **smoked wild salmon**

Put the asparagus in a steamer, cover, and cook for 5 minutes or until just tender.

Meanwhile, broil the hazelnuts in a foil-lined broiler pan until lightly browned. Whisk the oil, lime juice, and mustard together with a little salt and black pepper in a bowl, and then stir in the hot nuts. Keep warm.

Pour water into a saucepan to a depth of 1½ inches and bring it to a boil. Lower the eggs into the water with a slotted spoon and cook for 1 minute. Remove the pan from the heat and let the eggs stand for 1 minute. Drain the eggs, rinse with cold water, and drain again.

Tear the salmon into strips and divide the strips among 6 serving plates, folding and twisting the strips attractively. Tuck the just-cooked asparagus into the salmon, halve the quail eggs, leaving the shells on, if desired, and arrange them on top. Drizzle with the warm nut dressing, sprinkle with a little black pepper, and serve.

SMOKED HADDOCK & KALE SOUP

Haddock is a good source of brain-friendly omega-3s. Its smoky flavor works beautifully with the freshness of the kale.

Preparation time: 10 minutes
Cooking time: 25 minutes
Serves 4

....

1 tablespoon **olive oil**
2 **shallots**, diced
3 **garlic cloves**, crushed
1 large **potato**, peeled and diced
1½ cups **soymilk**
2 cups **water**
4½ cups shredded **kale**
10 oz smoked **haddock**, skinned and chopped
salt and **black pepper**

Heat the oil in a saucepan, add the shallots and garlic, and cook for 3 to 4 minutes or until softened. Add the potato, milk, and water and season to taste. Bring to a boil, then reduce the heat and simmer for about 5 to 6 minutes.

....

Stir the shredded kale into the mixture and cook for another 10 to 12 minutes or until the vegetables are tender. Stir in the chopped haddock and let simmer for 2 minutes or until cooked through.

....

Ladle the hot soup into 4 serving bowls and serve immediately.

....

SPICY CHARD & BEAN SOUP

Bursting with flavor, fiber, and nutrients, this is a filling soup that will boost concentration and cognition, while keeping blood-sugar levels steady.

Preparation time: 15 minutes
Cooking time: 25 minutes
Serves 4 to 6

2 tablespoons **olive oil**
2 **garlic cloves**, minced
2 **chiles**, seeded and minced
1 large **onion**, minced
1 large **carrot**, diced
1 **celery** stalk, diced
2 large bunches of **chard**, chopped
1 teaspoon **rosemary** leaves, chopped
1 teaspoon **thyme** leaves
2½ cups **chicken** or **vegetable stock**
1 (14 oz) can **chopped tomatoes**
1 (14 oz) can **kidney beans**, rinsed
and drained
¾ cup canned **lima beans**, rinsed
and drained
3½ oz **sun-dried tomatoes** in oil, chopped,
plus 2 tablespoons oil from the jar
sea salt and **black pepper**
small bunch of **basil**, torn, divided
finely grated zest of ½ **lemon**
plain live yogurt, to serve (optional)

Heat the olive oil in a large saucepan over medium heat and add the garlic cloves, chiles, and onion. Cook for 2 to 3 minutes, and then add the carrot, celery, chard, rosemary, and thyme. Cook for another 2 to 3 minutes, stirring frequently.

Add the stock, tomatoes, beans, and sun-dried tomatoes and bring to a boil. Reduce the heat and let simmer for 10 to 15 minutes or until the vegetables are tender.

Season to taste, then place 2 to 3 ladlesful of the soup in a food processor with the sun-dried tomato oil and half the basil. Blend until smooth then return to the pan. Add the remaining basil and the lemon zest, and then divide among serving bowls. Top each portion with a swirl of yogurt, if using.

PARSNIP, SAGE & CHESTNUT SOUP

The sage in this sophisticated soup will help boost brain power by improving your memory, concentration, and problem-solving skills.

Preparation time: 15 minutes
Cooking time: 50 minutes
Serves 4

3 tablespoons **chile oil**, plus extra for drizzling
40 **sage leaves**
1 **leek**, trimmed, cleaned, and chopped
4 **parsnips**, peeled and coarsely chopped
2½ pints **vegetable stock**
pinch of **ground cloves**
1 (7 oz) package cooked peeled **chestnuts**
2 tablespoons **lemon juice**
salt and **black pepper**
plain Greek yogurt, to serve

Heat the chile oil in a large saucepan over medium heat until a sage leaf placed in the chile oil sizzles and turns crisp after about 15 to 20 seconds. Add the remaining leaves, in batches, and fry until crisp. Lift them out of the saucepan with a slotted spoon and transfer to a plate lined with paper towels. Set aside.

Add the leek and parsnips to the pan and sauté gently for about 10 minutes, or until softened. Add the stock and cloves and bring to a boil. Reduce the heat, cover, and cook gently for 30 minutes, or until the vegetables are soft. Stir in the chestnuts and cook for another 5 minutes.

Blend the soup with a handheld stick blender or add the soup to a food processor, blend it, and return it to the pan. Stir in the lemon juice and reheat gently, seasoning to taste with salt and black pepper.

Ladle into 4 bowls, top with a spoonful of crème fraîche or Greek yogurt, and drizzle sparingly with extra chile oil to taste. Serve sprinkled with the sage leaves.

WALNUT-CRUSTED SALMON

With a double helping of omega-3 oils and a host of antioxidants, this tasty meal will send your brain power soaring. Try doing the crossword puzzle afterward!

Preparation time: 15 minutes
Cooking time: 10 to 15 minutes
Serves 4

4 (5 oz) **wild salmon fillets**
2 tablespoons **whole-grain mustard**
2 tablespoons **honey**
2 tablespoons chopped **tarragon**
1 cup finely chopped **walnuts**
sea salt and **black pepper**

Spinach salad
7 oz **baby spinach**
½ **cucumber**, chopped
handful of **cherry tomatoes**, halved
2 **scallions**, chopped
2 tablespoons **olive oil**, plus extra
for greasing
finely grated zest and juice of 1 **lemon**
handful of **pine nuts**, toasted
3½ oz **feta cheese**, diced
handful of **mint** leaves, chopped
1 **whole-wheat pita bread**, toasted
and torn into pieces

Place the salmon fillets, skinside down, on a lightly greased baking pan. Combine the mustard, honey, tarragon, and walnuts in a small bowl and season to taste.

Press the mixture evenly over the top and sides of the fillets and place in a preheated oven, at 350°F, for about 10 to 15 minutes or until the fish just flakes when pressed with a small knife.

Meanwhile, add the spinach, cucumber, cherry tomatoes, and scallions to a large bowl and toss them together. Drizzle with the olive oil, lemon juice and zest, and toss again. Mix in the pine nuts, feta, and mint. Divide the mixture among 4 plates and sprinkle with the toasted pita pieces. Set a salmon fillet onto each portion to serve.

BELL PEPPER, FETA & EGG TAGINE

This scrumptious Moroccan-influenced dish will shift your brain into top gear. Include a chopped chile if you like a bit of a kick.

Preparation time: 10 minutes
Cooking time: 15 to 20 minutes
Serves 4
....

2 tablespoons **olive oil**
1 teaspoon **cumin seeds**
1 teaspoon **coriander seeds**
1 each green, red, and yellow **bell pepper**, cored, seeded, and finely sliced
2 tablespoons pitted, halved **black olives**
5 oz **feta cheese**, cubed
4 **eggs**
black pepper
shredded **basil** leaves, to garnish
warm **whole-grain bread**, to serve (optional)

Heat the oil in a heavy skillet or the bottom of a tagine over medium-high heat. Stir in the cumin and coriander seeds, and cook for 1 to 2 minutes. Add the bell pepper slices and cook for another 2 to 3 minutes. Then stir in the olives. Cover, reduce the heat to medium, and cook for 5 minutes or until the bell pepper slices have softened.
....

Add the feta and cook for 2 to 3 minutes or until it begins to soften. Then make 4 wells in the mixture. Break the eggs into the wells, cover, and cook for 4 to 5 minutes, or until the whites are firm. Grind black pepper over the eggs, garnish with the basil leaves, and serve with warm crusty bread, if using.
....

SPICY CHICKEN WITH LEMON RICE

This energy-boosting meal is rich in brain nutrients, including turmeric, which is well known for its ability to improve memory and cognition.

Preparation time: 20 minutes
Cooking time: 40 to 45 minutes
Serves 4
················

2 **garlic cloves**, minced
⅓ cup **plain live yogurt**
1 teaspoon **paprika**
1 teaspoon **ground cumin**
1 teaspoon **ground turmeric**
½ teaspoon **ground cinnamon**
finely grated zest and juice of 1 **lime**
2 tablespoons **tomato paste**
1 tablespoon **olive oil**, plus extra
for brushing
4 (8 oz) boneless **chicken breasts**

Lemon rice
2¼ cups **brown rice**
2 tablespoons **butter**
1 **onion**, finely diced
1 teaspoon **ground turmeric**
finely grated zest and juice of 1 **lemon**
sea salt and **black pepper**

Put the garlic, yogurt, paprika, cumin, turmeric, cinnamon, lime juice and zest, tomato paste, and olive oil in a large bowl and mix well. Add the chicken breasts, stir to coat, and let marinate for 20 minutes.
···

Meanwhile, cook the brown rice in a saucepan of lightly salted boiling water, according to the package instructions, until tender. Rinse in hot water and drain.
···

Melt the butter in a large saucepan or wok over low heat, add the onion, and cook gently for 5 to 8 minutes, or until just soft. Stir in the turmeric, lemon zest and juice, and the cooked rice. Season to taste and cook gently, covered, for 3 to 5 minutes.
···

Heat a heavy skillet or ridged grill pan over high heat until very hot and brush with a little olive oil. Place the coated chicken breasts in the pan and cook for 3 to 4 minutes on each side until cooked through but still moist. Serve the chicken with the rice.
···

GINGER & LIME MACKEREL

Among its many health benefits, mackerel contains coenzyme Q10, which nourishes brain cells. It's the perfect food for eating yourself smart.

Preparation time: 15 minutes
Cooking time: 25 minutes
Serves 2

....

1 small **fennel bulb**, trimmed and sliced
8 **new potatoes**, thickly sliced
2 **tomatoes**, cut into wedges
2 tablespoons **olive oil**
½ teaspoon **fennel seeds**
2 whole **mackerel**
1 tablespoon **soy sauce**
½ inch piece of fresh **ginger root**, peeled and grated
finely grated zest and juice of 1 **lime**
1 teaspoon **honey**
salt and **black pepper**
lime wedges, to serve

Spread the fennel, potatoes, and tomatoes out on a baking sheet, drizzle with the oil, sprinkle with the fennel seeds, and season. Place in a preheated oven, at 400°F, for 25 minutes, turning occasionally, until cooked and lightly charred.

Meanwhile, slash the mackerel skin several times. Season both sides, and then place, skinside up, in a foil-lined broiler pan. Mix together the soy sauce, ginger, lime zest and juice, and honey in a small bowl and drizzle half of it over the fish.

Cook under a preheated hot broiler until the skin starts to crisp. Turn the fish over, drizzle with the remaining soy mixture, and broil for another 2 to 3 minutes, or until the mackerel is cooked through and flakes easily. Serve with the vegetables with lime wedges on the side.

....

CRISPY SALMON RAMEN

This nutritious Far Eastern broth topped with wild salmon will provide a boost for the brain and virtually every other organ.

Preparation time: 10 minutes
Cooking time: 15 minutes
Serves 2

....

2 teaspoons **peanut oil**
2 boneless **wild salmon fillets**, skin on
2 cups hot clear **chicken stock**
1 tablespoon **lime juice**
2 teaspoons **Thai fish sauce**
1 tablespoon **soy sauce**
¾ inch piece of fresh **ginger root**, peeled and cut into matchsticks
1 small **red chile**, thinly sliced
2 heads of **bok choy**, sliced in half lengthwise
5 oz **ramen** or **egg noodles**
cilantro leaves, to garnish

Put the oil into a large skillet over medium heat and fry the salmon fillets, skin-side down, for 3 to 5 minutes, or until the skin is crispy. Carefully turn the fillets over and cook for another minute, until still slightly rare. Transfer to a plate and keep warm.

Pour the stock into a saucepan, add the lime juice, fish sauce, soy sauce, and ginger and bring to a boil. Simmer for 3 to 4 minutes, then add the chile and bok choy. Let simmer for another 4 to 5 minutes, or until tender.

Meanwhile, cook the noodles in a saucepan of boiling water for 2 to 3 minutes according to the package instructions until just tender. Drain and pile into 2 bowls.

Ladle the hot stock over the noodles and top each bowl with a salmon fillet. Serve immediately, garnished with cilantro.

QUAIL WITH GINGER & GRAPES

An impressive dinner-party dish. You could use a mixture of grape varieties to make the plate look more colorful.

Preparation time: 10 minutes
Cooking time: 25 to 30 minutes
Serves 4

....

2 tablespoons **sunflower oil**
3 tablespoons **butter**
4 to 6 oven-ready **quail**
½ cup peeled and finely chopped fresh **ginger root**
3 **garlic cloves**, finely diced
1½ cups halved seedless **black grapes**
salt and **black pepper**
couscous or **quinoa**, to serve

Heat the oil and the butter in a large Dutch oven over medium heat. Add the quail and brown on both sides for 4 to 5 minutes, then transfer to a plate.

....

Stir the ginger and garlic into the pan, and cook for 1 to 2 minutes. Then toss in the grapes and season well. Return the quail to the pan, cover, and cook over medium heat for 20 minutes, or until cooked through. Serve with couscous on the side and a good grinding of black pepper over everything.

....

ESPRESSO & CHILI PORK TENDERLOIN

Rich in brain-boosting nutrients and fiber, this is a perfect dish to help you unwind at the end of the day.

Preparation time: 20 minutes, plus marinating
Cooking time: 25 minutes
Serves 4

2 teaspoons **instant espresso powder**
2 teaspoons **chili powder**
pinch of **cayenne pepper**
2 teaspoons **dark-brown sugar**
sea salt and **black pepper**
1 (2¼ lb) piece of **pork tenderloin**

Braised chard and leeks
3 tablespoons **olive oil**, plus extra for greasing
1 small **onion**, diced
1 **garlic clove**, crushed
2¼ lb **leeks**, sliced
1 lb **chard**, roughly torn

Combine the espresso powder, spices, and sugar in a small bowl with a pinch each of salt and pepper. Pat the pork dry with paper towels and place in a shallow bowl. Rub the spice mixture all over the pork, cover with plastic wrap, and let stand in the refrigerator for 8 hours or overnight to marinate. Return to room temperature before cooking.

For the vegetables, heat the olive oil in a large saucepan over low heat, add the onion and garlic, and cook for 5 to 8 minutes or until just soft. Add the leek slices and chard stalks, season to taste, cover, and bring to a simmer for 10 minutes, or until tender. Add the chard leaves, cover the saucepan again, and cook briefly until wilted.

Meanwhile, grease a large Dutch oven and place over medium heat until hot. Sear the outside of the pork pieces, turning from time to time, until browned all over. Transfer to a preheated oven, at 350°F, for about 15 minutes, or until just cooked through. Remove from the oven, cover loosely with the lid, and let rest for 10 minutes. To serve, slice the pork and place on a bed of braised chard and leeks drizzled with any cooking juices left behind in the Dutch oven.

LAMB WITH KALE & SPICY TOMATO SALSA

Kale packs more antioxidants, fiber, and omega-3s into its leaves than almost any other green vegetable, and it is delicious, too.

Preparation time: 10 minutes
Cooking time: 10 minutes
Serves 4

....

1 teaspoon **dried oregano**
2 tablespoons **olive oil**
1 teaspoon grated **lemon** zest
4 frenched **lamb rib chops**
4 cups coarsely sliced curly **kale**
salt and **black pepper**

Tomato salsa
2 large ripe **tomatoes**, seeded and diced
½ small **red onion**, finely diced
1 large **red chile**, finely diced
pinch of **sugar**
2 teaspoons **lemon juice**
1 tablespoon **olive oil**
2 tablespoons chopped **parsley**

Combine the oregano, olive oil, and lemon zest in a bowl with a pinch of salt and black pepper, and rub the mixture over the lamb chops. Arrange on a foil-lined broiler rack and put under a preheated hot broiler for 6 to 8 minutes or until cooked to your preference, turning once during cooking.

....

Meanwhile, cook the kale in a large saucepan of salted boiling water for 5 to 6 minutes or until tender.

....

Combine the salsa ingredients in a bowl and season to taste.

....

Pile the kale onto plates, then arrange a lamb chop on top. Serve with the salsa on the side.

....

CREMINI MUSHROOM PILAF

Mushrooms and brown rice are excellent sources of B vitamins, which help to energize your brain cells and relieve the impact of stress.

Preparation time: 10 minutes
Cooking time: 40 minutes
Serves 4
....

2 tablespoons **vegetable oil**
1 **onion**, finely diced
2 **garlic cloves**, minced
3 cups diced **cremini mushrooms**
3 **cardamom** pods, lightly crushed
¼ teaspoon **ground cloves**
½ teaspoon **ground cinnamon**
¾ cup **brown rice**
2 cups hot **vegetable stock**
salt and **black pepper**
1 cup **frozen peas**, defrosted
3 cups coarsely chopped **spinach**
fried **onions**, to garnish (optional)

Heat the oil in a large Dutch oven and cook the onion and garlic for 4 to 5 minutes over low heat, stirring occasionally, until they are beginning to brown.

....

Add the mushrooms, increase the heat to medium, and cook for 2 minutes. Then add the spices and rice and stir for 1 minute.

....

Pour in the stock, season generously, and cover tightly with the lid. Let simmer gently for about 15 minutes or until the rice grains are almost tender.

....

Remove from the heat, fold in the peas and spinach, and cover. Set aside to rest for 4 to 5 minutes, or until the liquid has been absorbed and the rice is tender.

....

Serve garnished with fried onions, if using.

....

FRAGRANT VEGETARIAN CHILI

This is a hearty, soothing meal to get your brain and nervous system firing on all cylinders.

Preparation time: 15 minutes
Cooking time: 30 to 40 minutes
Serves 4

2 tablespoons **olive oil**
1 large **onion**, chopped
2 **garlic cloves**, chopped
1 **red chile**, seeded and finely chopped
1 teaspoon **ground cumin**
1 **celery** stalk, chopped
2 large **sweet potatoes**,
peeled and cut into chunks
1 **red bell pepper**, cored, seeded,
and chopped
2 (14 oz) cans **cherry tomatoes**
in juice
2 tablespoons **tomato paste**
1¼ cups **vegetable stock**
7 oz small **button mushrooms**
1 (14 oz) can **kidney beans**,
rinsed and drained
2 handfuls of **kale**
sea salt and **black pepper**

To serve
quinoa
sour cream
chopped fresh **cilantro**
shredded **cheddar cheese**

Heat the olive oil in a large saucepan over low heat and add the onion, garlic, and chile. Cook gently for 5 to 8 minutes or until the onion is soft, then stir in the cumin, celery, sweet potatoes, and red bell pepper and cook for another 2 minutes.

Add the tomatoes, tomato paste, and stock and bring to a boil. Reduce the heat and let simmer for 15 minutes. Add the mushrooms, kidney beans, and kale to the saucepan and simmer for another 5 to 10 minutes or until the kale is tender. Season to taste and serve on a bed of quinoa. Add a spoonful of sour cream to each portion, sprinkle with cilantro and shredded cheddar, and serve .

SPAGHETTI WITH KALE & TOMATOES

This is a great midweek dinner—easy to prepare, and loaded with nutrients to help you unwind and enjoy your evening.

Preparation time: 15 minutes
Cooking time: 20 minutes
Serves 4

....

7 oz **spelt spaghetti**
2 tablespoons **olive oil**
1 small **red onion**, sliced
3 **garlic cloves**, finely diced
large bunch of **kale**, stalks removed
1⅓ cups quartered **cherry tomatoes**
sea salt and **black pepper**
3½ oz **pecorino cheese**, shredded, divided
small bunch of **basil**, torn, divided

Cook the spaghetti in a large saucepan of lightly salted boiling water according to the package instructions until tender.

....

Meanwhile, heat the oil in a large, heavy skillet over low heat, add the onion and garlic, and cook for 5 to 8 minutes or until soft. Add the kale, raise the heat to medium and cook, stirring, for another 5 minutes. Add the cherry tomatoes, season to taste, and cook for a further 5 minutes.

....

Drain the spaghetti and add to the kale and tomato mixture with a little of the cooking water. Toss to coat. Stir in three-quarters of the cheese and half of the basil. Divide among 4 serving plates and sprinkle with the remaining cheese and basil, along with a grinding of black pepper, to serve.

....

BAKED PUMPKIN, BEETS & CHEESE

You can choose your favorite vegetables for this tasty baked dish, but remember to include beets for their antioxidant power and generous levels of iron.

Preparation time: 20 minutes
Cooking time: 25 to 30 minutes
Serves 4

....

5 raw **beets**, peeled and diced
½ **butternut squash** or 1¼ lb of **pumpkin**, peeled, seeded, and cut into small wedges or diced slightly larger than the beet dice
1 **red onion**, cut into wedges
2 tablespoons **olive oil**
2 teaspoons **fennel seeds**
salt and **black pepper**
2 (3½ oz) **goat cheese**
chopped **rosemary**, to garnish

Put all the vegetables into a roasting pan, drizzle with the oil, sprinkle with the fennel seeds and season with the salt and pepper. Roast in a preheated oven, at 400°F, for 20 to 25 minutes, turning once, or until well browned and tender.

....

Cut the goat cheese into thirds and nestle it among the roasted vegetables. Season the cheese wedges with a little salt and black pepper and drizzle with some of the pan juices.

....

Return the pan to the oven and cook for about 5 minutes or until the cheese is just beginning to melt. Scatter with chopped rosemary and serve immediately.

....

BEAN BURGERS WITH PECAN COLESLAW

These spicy bean burgers can be made in advance and frozen for a nutritious, last-minute meal.

Preparation time: 25 minutes
Cooking time: 10 minutes
Serves 4

2 (14 oz) cans **kidney beans**, rinsed and drained
1 **red chile**, seeded and finely chopped
1 **egg**
1 **tomato**, chopped
1 **scallion**, chopped
1 cup **whole-wheat bread crumbs**
1 teaspoon **ground cumin**
½ teaspoon **ground cinnamon**
oil, for greasing
sea salt and **black pepper**
4 **whole-grain burger buns**, to serve

Coleslaw
½ small **white cabbage**, shredded
2 **Granny Smith apples**, grated
¾ cup **pecans**, lightly toasted and chopped
1 cup **black grapes**, thinly sliced
1 **red onion**, very thinly sliced
1 tablespoon **caraway seeds**, lightly toasted
2 tablespoons chopped fresh **cilantro**
½ cup good-quality **mayonnaise**
2 tablespoons **plain live yogurt**
finely grated zest and juice of 1 **lemon**
1 tablespoon **honey**
sea salt and **black pepper**

Put all of the burger ingredients in a food processor, season to taste, and process until just combined. Using your hands, shape the mixture into 4 large patties and place them on a lightly greased nonstick baking sheet. Cook the patties under a preheated hot broiler for 5 minutes on each side or until sizzling and golden.

For the coleslaw, put the cabbage, apple, pecans, grapes, and onion in a large bowl and toss together to mix. Add the remaining ingredients to a small bowl, season to taste, and beat together to make a dressing. Pour over the vegetables and toss to coat. Serve the coleslaw in the buns with the burgers.

COFFEE GRANITA & VANILLA YOGURT

This light dessert is perfect if you still have work to do in the evening. But even if you don't, the yogurt helps to soothe and relax after a long day.

Preparation time: 15 minutes, plus cooling and freezing
Serves 4
....

½ cup **turbinado sugar**
1 oz **unsweetened chocolate**, grated, plus extra to decorate
2½ cups hot **espresso coffee**
1¼ cups **plain live yogurt**
seeds scraped from 1 **vanilla bean**
1 tablespoon **powdered sugar**

Stir the sugar and chocolate into the hot coffee until dissolved. Let cool then pour into a shallow dish and place in the freezer for about 40 minutes. Use a fork to mix the ice crystals with the liquid then return to the freezer until the mixture is fully frozen, mixing again every 15 minutes.
....

Meanwhile, combine the live yogurt, vanilla seeds, and powdered sugar in a bowl and place in the freezer for about 20 minutes. Using an electric beater or stand mixer, whip the mixture in order to aerate it. Divide the granita among 4 cups or dessert dishes and spoon some yogurt mixture on top of each. Decorate with a grating of dark chocolate, and serve.
....

COFFEE DESSERTS

Make your after-dinner conversation sparkle with these elegant desserts. The caffeine encourages the release of dopamine to boost your mood.

Preparation time: 10 minutes
Serves 6

....

4 teaspoons **instant espresso powder**
2 tablespoons boiling **water**
1 cup **mascarpone cheese**
3 tablespoons **powdered sugar**
1 cup heavy **whipping cream**
unsweetened **cocoa powder**, for dusting
6 **chocolate-covered coffee beans**, to decorate
cantuccini or **amaretti cookies**, to serve

Put the espresso powder in a heatproof bowl with the water, stir to dissolve, and let cool slightly.

....

Put the mascarpone and powdered sugar in another bowl and add the coffee. Beat the mixture using a hand-held electric beater, or in a stand mixer, until smooth.

....

Whip the cream using a handheld electric beater, or in a stand mixer, until it forms soft peaks. Then gently fold two-thirds of the cream into the coffee mixture. Divide the mixture among 6 espresso cups or small glasses, then top with the remaining cream.

....

Dust each portion with cocoa powder and decorate with a coffee bean on top. Serve immediately with the cookies.

....

COFFEE & WALNUT CAKE

Rich, light, and full of flavor, this cake packs a host of B vitamins, antioxidants, and omega-3 oils to support your brain.

Preparation time: 25 minutes, plus cooling
Cooking time: 25 minutes
Makes 10 slices

....

1 tablespoon **instant espresso powder** or granules
1 tablespoon boiling **water**
1½ sticks (¾ cup) **butter**, softened, plus a little extra for greasing
¾ cup plus 2 tablespoons **superfine sugar**
3 **eggs**
1⅓ cups **all-purpose flour**
2 teaspoons **baking powder**
½ cup **walnuts**, finely chopped, plus extra walnut halves to decorate

Buttercream
1 teaspoon **instant espresso powder** or granules
2 teaspoons boiling **water**
1 stick (½ cup) **unsalted butter**, softened
1¼ cups **powdered sugar**, sifted

Dissolve the coffee powder in the water and set aside. Grease 2 (7-inch) cake pans and line the bottom of each pan with nonstick parchment paper.

....

Beat together the butter, sugar, eggs, flour, and baking powder in a mixing bowl until pale and creamy. Stir in the dissolved coffee and fold in the chopped walnuts.

....

Divide the batter evenly between the prepared cake pans and level the surface using a metal spatula. Bake in a preheated oven, at 350°F, for 25 minutes or until just firm to the touch. Loosen the edges, invert onto a wire rack, and peel off the lining paper. Let cool.

....

Make the buttercream. Dissolve the coffee powder in the water. Beat together the butter, powdered sugar, and dissolved coffee in a bowl until smooth and creamy. Use half of the buttercream to sandwich the cake halves together, then spread the remaining buttercream evenly over the top. Decorate with the reserved walnut halves.

....

ORANGE & CHOCOLATE TART

This bittersweet tart is truly delectable, and the flavonols in the chocolate will boost blood circulation to the brain, creating a real feel-good factor.

Preparation time: 30 minutes, plus chilling and cooling
Cooking time: 35 to 40 minutes
Serves 8 to 10

8 oz **semisweet chocolate**, broken into pieces
1 stick (½ cup) **butter**
2 **eggs**
2 **egg yolks**
⅓ cup **superfine sugar**
¼ cup fine-cut **orange marmalade**

Pastry dough
⅓ cup **powdered sugar**
2 cups **all-purpose flour**
1 stick (½ cup) cold **butter**, cubed
1 **egg**, beaten
finely grated zest of 1 **orange**
pinch of **salt**

For the pastry dough, sift the powdered sugar and flour into a bowl, add the butter, and rub it in with your fingertips until the mixture resembles fine bread crumbs. Add the egg, orange zest, and salt and mix to a soft dough. Seal in plastic wrap and let chill in the fridge for 20 minutes.

Roll out the dough on a lightly floured work surface and use it to line a 9-inch tart pan or pie plate. Chill for 30 minutes. Trim off the excess dough, then line the tart with nonstick parchment paper and fill it with dried beans or pastry weights. Bake in a preheated oven, at 400°F, for 10 minutes. Remove the paper and beans. Bake for another 10 minutes, or until crisp and golden. Let cool. Reduce the oven temperature to 350°F.

Melt the chocolate and butter in a heatproof bowl over a saucepan of barely simmering water, making sure that the water does not touch the base of the bowl. Once melted, let cool slightly. Beat the eggs, egg yolks, and sugar in a bowl until light and fluffy, then stir in the cooled chocolate mixture.

Spread the marmalade over the tart crust, and pour in the chocolate mixture. Bake in the oven for 15 to 20 minutes or until just set. Let cool.

CHOCOLATE-DIPPED STRAWBERRIES

Stress-relieving, full of fiber, and rich in brain-friendly nutrients, this is a dessert you can definitely justify eating.

Preparation time: 10 minutes, plus chilling
Cooking time: 5 minutes
Serves 4

1 tablespoon **instant espresso powder**
seeds scraped from 1 **vanilla bean**
1 lb **strawberries**
5 oz **semisweet chocolate**

Using a mortar and pestle, grind the espresso powder with the vanilla seeds, until smooth. Arrange the strawberries on a cookie sheet lined with nonstick parchment paper and sprinkle half the coffee mixture over them. Turn the strawberries over and repeat.

Melt the chocolate in a heatproof bowl set over a pan of barely simmering water, making sure that the water does not touch the base of the bowl. Stir until smooth and glossy.

Hold a strawberry by its stalk and dip it in the chocolate, twisting the berry to coat about three-quarters of it in the chocolate. Return to the cookie sheet and repeat with the rest of the strawberries. Chill in the refrigerator for 10 minutes until the chocolate is firm.

CHOCOLATE AVOCADO PUDDING

The brain-boosting nutrients in this rich little dessert will work through the night to help put you on top form the next day.

Preparation time: 10 minutes, plus chilling
Cooking time: 5 minutes
Serves 4 to 6

....

5 oz **semisweet chocolate**
1 cup sweetened **hazelnut milk**
2 ripe **avocados**, peeled,
seeded, and chopped
1 tablespoon **unsweetened cocoa powder**
2 teaspoons **vanilla extract**
½ teaspoon **ground cinnamon**
pinch of **sea salt**
sliced **strawberries** or **raspberries**, to serve

Melt the chocolate in a heatproof bowl over a pan of barely simmering water, ensuring that the water does not touch the base of the bowl. Stir until smooth and glossy.

....

Put the chocolate in a food processor with all the remaining ingredients, except the berries, and blend until smooth and creamy. Spoon into individual glasses or ramekins and let chill for at least 2 hours. Scatter each portion with berries just before serving.

....

CINNAMON-BAKED APPLES

High in fiber, these spicy apples will keep blood-sugar levels steady and get your brain cells in gear.

Preparation time: 10 minutes
Cooking time: 30 minutes
Serves 4

....

2 tablespoons **brown sugar**
1 teaspoon **ground cinnamon**
1 teaspoon **ground ginger**
½ teaspoon grated **nutmeg**
⅔ cup **golden raisins**
½ teaspoon **vanilla extract**
4 **Granny Smith apples**, cored
1 teaspoon **butter**
1 **star anise**
2 **cinnamon sticks**
1 **vanilla bean**, bruised
½ cup pressed **apple juice**
plain live yogurt, to serve

Add the sugar, cinnamon, ginger, nutmeg, golden raisins, and vanilla extract to a small bowl and stir to combine. Stuff the mixture into the cavities of the apples and stand them upright in a baking dish. Dot a little butter on top of each apple and place the star anise, cinnamon sticks, and vanilla bean around them.

....

Pour the juice in around the apples, cover with foil, and place in a preheated oven, at 350°F, for 30 minutes or until the apples are soft and starting to collapse. Serve cold or warm, drizzled with any juices from the baking dish, and a spoonful of plain live yogurt on the side.

....

FRUIT PACKAGES & PISTACHIO YOGURT

For this, use your favorite seasonal fruits in all different colors; the brighter the better. Fruit salad never tasted so good!

Preparation time: 10 minutes,
Cooking time: 10 minutes
Serves 2

....

1 cup mixed **blueberries** and **raspberries**
2 **peaches** or **nectarines**, halved, pitted, and sliced
½ **cinnamon stick**, halved
1 tablespoon **honey**
2 tablespoons **orange juice**
3 tablespoons chopped and shelled **pistachio nuts**, plus a few whole kernels, to decorate
¼ cup **plain Greek yogurt**

Cut 2 large, double-thickness squares of foil. Divide the fruit and cinnamon between the squares and drizzle with honey and orange juice. Fold the foil over the filling and pinch the edges together to seal.

....

Place the fruit packages on a barbecue or under a preheated medium broiler for about 10 minutes or until the fruit is soft and hot.

....

Meanwhile, mix the chopped nuts with the yogurt in a bowl and set aside. Open the foil packages, transfer the fruit to serving bowls, and scatter each serving with a few pistachio kernels. Spoon the yogurt mixture over the warm fruit to serve.

....

BLUEBERRY & DATE MOUSSE

This light, creamy dessert is so totally yummy you would never believe it's good for you, but it's packed with antioxidant power.

Preparation time: 10 minutes
Serves 4

....

½ cup **dates**
½ cup pitted **prunes**
grated zest of 1 **orange**
2 tablespoons **crème fraîche**
3 to 4 tablespoons **plain live yogurt**
⅔ cup **blueberries**
grated **semisweet chocolate**, to serve

Put the dates and pitted prunes into a food processor along with the orange zest and blend until broken down.

....

Add into the processor the crème fraîche, yogurt, and blueberries and blend again until you have a mousse-like texture.

....

Spoon into 4 glasses and sprinkle with some grated chocolate to serve.

....

FROZEN BERRY YOGURT

This refreshing, nutrient-loaded dessert is quick, easy, and, if you haven't got time, equally delicious served chilled not frozen.

Preparation time: 15 minutes, plus freezing
Serves 4 to 6
....

1⅔ cups **strawberries**, hulled
1⅔ cups **blueberries**
1 teaspoon **vanilla extract**
⅓ cup **agave syrup**
½ cup **demerara sugar**
1¼ cups **plain live yogurt**

Put all the ingredients in a food processor and blend until smooth. Pour into a shallow dish and place in the freezer for 1 hour.
....

Use a handheld electric beater to beat the mixture until smooth. Then return it to the freezer for another hour until frozen. Let it stand at room temperature until slightly softened before serving.
....

APPLE, MAPLE & PECAN WHIPS

The sharpness of Granny Smith apples combined with the sweetness of maple syrup and the toasty pecans make this dessert a real winner.

Preparation time: 10 minutes, plus cooling
Cooking time: 5 minutes
Serves 4

....

¾ cup good-quality **applesauce**
1 **Granny Smith apple**, peeled and grated or finely chopped
1 cup **heavy cream**
1 cup store-bought **vanilla pudding**
3 tablespoons **maple syrup**
¼ cup **pecans**, toasted and chopped
pecan cookies, to serve

Put the applesauce and apple into a small saucepan. Cook for 5 minutes to soften, then add to a metal bowl and place in the freezer for a few minutes to cool.

....

Whip the cream until soft peaks form, then stir in the pudding. Swirl through the maple syrup and applesauce, and then spoon the mixture into 4 teacups or dishes. Sprinkle with toasted pecans and serve with pecan cookies on the side.

....

RESOURCES

Alzheimer's Association
Helpline: (800) 272-3900
Email: info@alz.org
Website: www.alz.org

Alzheimer's Foundation of America
Tel: (866) 232-8484 (Toll free)
Website: www.alzfdn.org

American Chronic Pain Association
Tel: (800) 533 3231
Website: www.theacpa.org

American Foundation for Suicide Prevention
Tel: (888) 333-2377
Email: info@afsp.org
Website: www.afsp.org

American Heart Association
Tel: (800) 242-8721
Website: www.heart.org

The American Institute of Stress
Tel: (682) 239-6823
Email: info@stress.org
Website: www.stress.org

American Meditation Society
Website: americanmeditationsociety.org

American Nutrition Association
Website: americannutritionassociation.org

American Yoga Association
Email: info@americanyogaassociation.org
Website: americanyogaassociation.org

Anxiety and Depression Association of America
Tel: (240) 485 1001
Website: www.adaa.org

Brain & Behavior Research Foundation
Tel: (800) 829-8289
Website: www.bbrfoundation.org

Diabetes Action
Tel: (202) 333-4520
Email: info@diabetesaction.org
Website: www.diabetesaction.org

Insomnia Land
Website: www.insomnialand.com

Mayo Clinic
Website: www.mayoclinic.org/healthy-living/
stress-management/resources/HLV-20049495

Mental Health America
Tel: (800) 969-6642 (Toll free)
Website: www.mentalhealthamerica.net

Mental Health and Addiction Network
Tel: (617) 949-0030
Website: www.mhfederation.org

Substance Abuse and Mental Health Services Administration
Website: www.findtreatment.samhsa.gov
(Behavioral Health Treatment Services Locator)

**World's Healthiest Foods
(George Mateljan Foundation)**
Website: www.whfoods.org

INDEX

ACKNOWLEDGMENTS

Getty Images Larry Washburn 30. **Shutterstock** amphaiwan 15 above; Andre Bonn 5; Andris Tkacenko 9; bonchan 7; nanka 23; pkstock 8; Scisetti Alfio 27; Shawn Hempel 10. **Thinkstock** Alexandru Dobrea 12; Edward Westmacott 25; kone 15 below; Natikka 17; Watcha 28.